SHIP AND SHORE: AN INSIDER EXPLAINS THE MARITIME WORLD

SHIP AND SHORE: AN INSIDER EXPLAINS THE MARITIME WORLD

David Reid

CONTENTS

DEDICATION

To all the seafarers who have served and continue to sail the oceans to sustain the global supply chain.

A special thank you to my wife Ann, whose everlasting support and encouragement made this book possible.

INTRODUCTION

Embracing Change

In 1968, I made a decision that would change my life. I remember the surprise when I informed my parents that I had decided to join the British Merchant Navy. There was no tradition of seafaring in our family history; my parents and grandparents had all been either craftsmen or shopkeepers. I was studying mechanical engineering at a North London technical college and for years had aspired to become a civil engineer. When I made the abrupt change of course to head off to sea, I still intended to. I planned to use seafaring as a form of sabbatical, traveling at someone else's expense and returning after a few years to resume my engineering study. Entering new territory can have unexpected consequences, however: 50 years later I have yet to start my civil engineering career.

In my work as a port chaplain with the Seafarers' Church Institute (SCI) in the Port of Philadelphia, I have conversations with navigating officers from around the globe. After they find out that I have also served as a chief officer, they often ask me how I made the transition from serving at sea to working ashore. This subject is at the front of many seafarers' minds as they weigh continuing their career against spending more months away from home and family.

"How do I secure a shore-based job?" A young Filipino captain who had recently taken his first command on a car carrier posed the question to me as I was driving him into downtown Philadelphia. He had not been ashore for two months and needed some time to reset by visiting the Liberty Bell among the tourists.

I told him that, first, he needed to think about what would be next and prepare for the changes that would come with it. I had decided that, after eight years at sea and reaching the rank of chief officer, my future was not to remain a seafarer. To realize the change, I decided to volunteer for any job that nobody else wanted. The Canadian shipping company that employed me had a fleet of self-unloaders and bulk carriers operating in difficult trades. I let them know that I was open to any challenge that they had.

The Filipino captain wanted to know how I handled those difficult assignments. I explained that my first lesson in Royal Navy seamanship training, taught by a former chief petty officer, was that 90% of seamanship is common sense. His explanation involved a colorful story about dogs not requiring sex education. As I sought to find a shore job, I realized that I could take on other challenging tasks by applying that simple rule.

As a navigator, I trained to embrace change by planning for it. The second officer on a merchant vessel is responsible for voyage planning. The route is pulled together from a wide range of factors, including load-lines and forecasted weather, productivity and safe passage. Navigators have to think in four dimensions: latitude, longitude, depth and time. They know that during a voyage the actual conditions will often vary from the expected and build that variance into their plans. The mind of the watchkeeper is always running through alternate scenarios to make sure that, when circumstances shift, change can be embraced rather than feared.

Trading in the Gulf of St Lawrence, I learned that working during the winter months was entirely different from summer. We were navigating not by the shortest route, but by the location of open water and the movement of the ice pack. At times we would sit for days trapped in the ice, waiting for the pressure to abate so that we could move. The temperatures would drop to extremely low levels, and outside cabins would begin to chill as the ship's heating system failed to keep up. When we arrived at our loading port in Sept-Îles, Québec, we did not attempt to put out mooring lines; it was simply not possible due to the cold temperature, so the harbor tugs just held us against the pier while we loaded our cargo of iron ore. These changing conditions are only one example of the adaptability used by seafarers to cope.

In large corporations, creative thought is often stifled by the management's desire for policy to control every internal action. Onboard a ship, seafarers are also bound by a rule-based process that dictates by statute everything from how to avoid collisions to record-keeping requirements. The rules do not cover all the variables that seafarers will encounter, however: they have to continuously assess and make choices based on the intersection of regulatory guidance with what they are actually experiencing. They are small collaborative teams, living and working in a changing environment to which they have to adapt continually.

Officers are trained to become what American political historian James MacGregor Burns called 'transformational leaders'.[1] The hierarchy onboard a merchant ship results in leaders who have to rise up through the ranks. The career path for cadets is to gain experience and to pass examinations that will move them up the hierarchical ladder to become a junior officer and eventually to either a senior position or command onboard. By the time they are leaders, seafarers have received a holistic view of how each crewmember performs their critical part in the ship's overall performance and do well not to forget it.

I am fortunate to have served under such leaders who mentored and coached me. I remember very well Alistair, a second officer on my first ship who was from Zimbabwe (then called Rhodesia). He explained the mechanics of celestial navigation to me. A few years later, the skills I learned under Alistair's guidance got me named 'cadet of the year'. This is the power of transformational leadership, and it continues today onboard the ships that I visit as a chaplain. As I listen to the seafarers talk, I can detect in the ambiance of their conversation how they continue to adapt to change and the importance of transformational leadership onboard their ships. It is the special connection that lets seafarers think and function together, even when on paper great differences seem to separate one from the other.

This book plots a course of discovery through the lives of seafarers, the shipping industry and the past 50 years of change in it. Each of its chapters, which can be read in sequence or independently, covers a key topic in the unique world of the global seaborne supply chain. It is the product of four years of writing, and several of its chapters are based on articles first published in the North American Maritime Ministry Association (NAMMA)'s *The MARE Report*. The majority of the writing, however, took place over the summer of 2021, not long after I learned that the aortic valve in my heart needed to be replaced.

I had learned a few years earlier that my valve had been defective from birth. By May of 2021, the valve was failing and my physical energy level had reduced significantly. I was scheduled for open-heart surgery in late June and was determined to complete as much writing as possible beforehand, as such surgery is not without risks. I am pleased to report that it went very well, and in the early weeks of my recovery at a special cardiac clinic, I had the time needed to reflect and write the last few chapters.

As a former mariner, former port sector CEO and present port chaplain, my aim with this book is to impart some of my knowledge and perspective on all things maritime, from Marconi men to dockers to cabotage legislation. I especially hope it informs the work of my colleagues around the world promoting the social welfare of seafarers.

David Reid, MA FNI
November 2021

Navigating Cadet David Reid, 1968.

NOTES

1. James MacGregor Burns, 1978. *Leadership*. New York: Harper
    & Row.

PART I

ONBOARD SHIPS

CREW AND THE HIERARCHY ON SHIPS

Four Stripes

Master with stripes. Seamen's Church Institute
flickr.

Many mariners compare the role of the captain on board
a ship to a god or supreme being: the ultimate authority.
On a merchant ship, however, there is technically no rank
or qualification called 'captain'. Instead, this is the master
mariner. In the 2020 movie *Greyhound*, Tom Hanks plays the
captain of a US Navy destroyer on convoy duty in the North
Atlantic during World War II. The burden of command is
very much on display when Hanks takes evasive action to
protect the convoy of merchant ships from the prowling
threat of German submarines. *Greyhound* illustrates the
loneliness of command and is an accurate portrayal.

Ever since the Vikings set forth across the oceans, ships
have always had a hierarchical command structure led by a
single individual. The Norwegian *Gulating* law, dating back
to the 11th century, prescribed the role and duties of the
styrimaðr 'steerman', the skipper or master of a longship. On
a modern merchant ship, the ultimate authority on board

for all matters rests with the master. When in uniform, they wear four gold stripes on the arms of their jacket or the epaulets on each shoulder.

The safe navigation of a ship requires round-the-clock attention, and the navigation team, consisting of the deck officers, divides the day into periods of duty known as 'watches'. The members of the navigation team are also referred to as 'watchkeepers'. Typically, merchant ships operate on a 3-watch system, each watch lasting 4 hours and repeating twice in 24 hours. The chief mate takes the 4-8 watch, the second mate the 12-4 watch, and the third mate (the most junior) the 8-12. This system allows the master to oversee the watch of the most junior mate during hours that are convenient to the master.

Mates have qualifications that certify their competency to perform their tasks. Becoming a mate involves a combination of academic and practical training through a cadetship program. During the time serving as a cadet, the individual gains experience through mentoring and hands-on learning. Navigating cadet is the starting point from which every master in command originally rose.

Master of the *Titanic* Edward J. Smith. Public Domain.

Not all cadets will become a master, and the mathematics are such that this is not possible. Some find that they are content to remain serving as a mate. The burden of responsibility that comes with the four stripes is not for everyone. Others serve at sea for a limited period of time and then seek employment ashore that does not require long periods away from home. The effect of this natural attrition is that those who have both aspiration and aptitude rise steadily through the hierarchical system and eventually become appointed to serve as master, thereby earning their four stripes. The timeline for this process is governed by statutory periods of sea time served. It takes at least seven years and often longer.

Engineers

The structure of manning on a merchant ship has adapted with the technological evolution from wind power to propellers driven by engines. Under sail, the ship's complement revolved around the management of sails and navigation; thus, seamanship was the primary focus. The 19th century brought about the technological revolution from sail to propeller. The arrival of steam boilers, engines and their associated equipment introduced a new department onboard: the engineering department.

In the earliest stages, 'engineering' involved shoveling coal into boilers, but over time the task of operating the propulsion became more efficient. The engine room required around-the-clock attention, so the engineers were initially organized as watchkeepers in a mirror image of the mates. The professional engineers required academic training and qualifications and performed the task of managing the stokers, oilers, wipers and fitters.

Automation in the engine room has since changed the need for a physical presence and has reduced the level of manning needed. Instead, the engineers are on call to respond to alarms, and the rest of the time they work a normal day watch. The leader of the engineers has the title of chief engineer and wears four stripes, but since 1865, they have an additional purple stripe that differentiates them from the master. The chief engineer reports directly to the master and, in many respects, is equivalent to the chief mate as head of their own department. The career path for a chief engineer also commences with an engineering cadetship, just like the deck cadetship that leads to master.

The Galley

The deck and engineering departments are the two principal departments onboard a ship, with the master in command and the chief mate and chief engineer reporting directly to them. However, another department also reports to the master, and that is the catering department. The task of keeping the entire ship's complement fed and healthy rests with this small department, which often consists only of a cook and a messman.

Some might argue that the catering department is the real engine that keeps everyone sustained at sea. Meals need to be ready on time to match the watchkeeper's schedules, and the food has to be nutritious and in line with both the minimum victualling requirements and the ship manager's budget. The ordering and taking on of provisions and stores at each port of call requires forward planning and knowledge of availability in the countries where the ship is trading. Once the ship sets off, there is no opportunity to run to a convenience store, so the business of provisioning requires perfect planning so that nothing runs out mid-voyage.

The Team

The ship's complement is the hierarchical structure at the top: the master, the chief mate and the chief engineer. Within each department, the mates and engineers make up the deck and engineer officers. At the next level in each department, there are the ratings: these are the team of skilled and less-skilled persons who run the ship.

The term 'rating' evolved from the classification of crew members under the officers by their level of competence. On the engineering side, the team is small due to automation and may consist only of technicians and fitters performing routine maintenance and repairs. On the deck side, the ratings perform essential tasks such as handling mooring ropes at berthing, setting the pilot ladder, rigging the gangway and manually steering the ship under pilotage. They also undertake numerous maintenance and repair tasks. In port, the ratings act as security on the gangway watch. In emergencies, the ratings work as a team to deal with fire on board and launch lifeboats. The senior rating is the bo'sun or boatswain, a skilled seaman who leads and manages the team of ordinary seamen and deckhands.

Technology has eliminated the radio department, often known as 'sparks' or the 'Marconi man'. The radio officer held a crucial position in the era of morse code communication, but the arrival of satellites eliminated the need for transmission via the morse code key and, along with it, the individual that operated that key.[1]

Uniform

Merchant Navy uniforms became the fashion for British merchant mariners after World War I; this followed the title of 'Merchant Navy', bestowed by King George V in honor of the service and sacrifice of commercial merchant shipping. 3,000 British merchant ships had gone down during the Great War, with the loss of 15,000 merchant seamen.

When I first went to sea as a navigating cadet in November of 1968; I had to fly to Houston, Texas, to join my first ship, the London Prestige. Under the misguided impression that I was required to wear my uniform while traveling to join my ship, I boarded my transatlantic flight to New York at London Heathrow fully attired in my dress blues and cap.

As I boarded the plane, the flight attendant asked me if I worked for the airline; apparently, my uniform was similar to that of BOAC (the predecessor to British Airways). I found my seat, and within a few minutes, there was a tap on my shoulder, and a man in plain clothes asked me if I was joining the London Prestige. I was surprised. How could he know? Then I realized that my uniform was the giveaway.

That was the first and only time that I joined a ship in uniform!

The hierarchical structure on board a ship is universal, irrespective of flag state or crew nationality. Indeed, the system functions on a multi-national basis, often bringing together a master, officers and ratings of multiple nations who work together in a collaborative environment. The chain of command sets in place clear lines of responsibility and authority and is essential for the safety of all on board. No matter the flag, port of registry, or classification society, when a pilot steps onboard, it will always be the person with four stripes that welcomes them to the bridge.

NOTES

1. See the chapter 'Radio and Connecting Seafarers'.

2

SHIP CONSTRUCTION

Many Parts

Illustration of some shipbuilding methods in England, 1858. Public Domain.

The last 50 years have seen worldwide shipbuilding relocate almost entirely from Europe to Asia. One of the biggest changes came in the 1990s, when China started taking advantage of its strengths in steelmaking, heavy industry and low labor costs. China rapidly became the center for the construction of basic merchant ships, while Japan and South Korea took over the construction of more sophisticated specialty merchant ships. While all this was happening in Asia, the European yards were closing their doors. The only shipbuilding left in Europe is specialty ships for cruising, naval defense ships and the smaller coastal ships needed for short-range trade with other European countries.

Constructing something as massive as a boat to sustainably float on water takes lots of specialized components. The naval architects who design ships and the shipowners they work with are constantly looking for new cost-saving technologies and designs, so the specifics of construction are always changing. Often these have colorful names that reflect their unique maritime heritage.

Merchant ships are designed to carry different kinds of cargo. That cargo may be liquid or dry, free flowing in bulk, or in units or individual pieces of cargo, and all these need different kinds of ship construction. There are many things that are common to all ships, however, beginning with the bow.

The Bow

The bow section of every ship has a forecastle, anchors, windlasses, space for stores and chain lockers. The forecastle 'fo'c'sle', is the raised deck on the bow. On the fo'c'sle is kept the windlass, the anchor handling equipment with a special notched wheel called the 'gypsy' that feeds the anchor cables in and out of the vessel. The port and starboard anchors rest outside the hull, while the cables that attach them to the vessel are stored below the windlass in the chain locker, fastened to its bottom or 'bitter end'. The bitter end is designed to be released or break free in an emergency.

The cable feeds up from the chain locker to the fo'c'sle through the Spurling pipe, which is directly beneath the windlass, and then down from the fo'c'sle to the anchor outside through the Hawse pipe, which is near the tip of the hull. The anchor cable is often coated with mud and silt when it is winched in, so water jets are located in the Hawse pipe to wash it as it passes through. Not all of the mud and silt is removed, however, and some drains through the floor of the chain locker into the 'mud box' below. The mud box space is accessible for cleaning and can be pumped out via a bilge line. My least favorite job as a cadet was crawling inside to clean the mud box. It was not a place for anyone with even a mild case of claustrophobia. Below the mud box, there is a large ballast tank known as the 'fore peak tank'. This tank is only used for water ballast and is very useful for keeping the ship trimmed, balancing the angle of immersion between the bow and the stern.

The Main Body

The bow section of a ship is separated from the main body by the collision bulkhead, which is designed to protect the main body of the ship from a collision. Behind that collision bulkhead the business of every ship is found.

On a tanker, there are many tanks configured for oil or chemicals and separate water ballast tanks. Tankers also have networks of piping and valves for pumping cargo out to shore facilities. All of the operations are managed remotely from the ship's cargo control room. In the control room, tank valves are opened and closed, levels monitored, and pumps configured.

On a bulk carrier, the main body of the hull is divided into cargo holds by watertight bulkheads. Bulk cargo is loaded and discharged via hatch openings, which are primarily opened and closed using hydraulics and sit elevated above the deck on a vertical wall known as the hatch coaming. Hatch covers are often called 'MacGregors' after the company that leads in manufacturing them.

Access for dockers and longshoremen into the cargo holds is by ladders. There are two types: the straight vertical ladder and the 'Australian' ladder. The Australian ladder is a requirement for any ship trading at Australian ports and places a 20 ft limit on the maximum height of a vertical ladder, so it has platforms or sets of steps to break up the vertical climb. Under the Safety of Life at Sea (SOLAS) Convention, every hold must have two means of access: one at each end of the hold. Typically, one will be an Australian design and the other a vertical ladder. Remember that on a Panamax-size bulk carrier, the height of the cargo holds is maybe 18 m or 60 ft, a substantial climb on a vertical ladder.

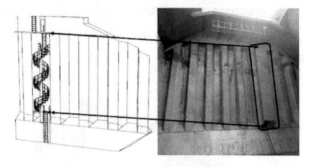

Enclosed Australian ladder on board *La Donna I.* Courtesy of the La Donna I *Casualty Investigation Report*, Republic of the Marshall Islands Maritime Administrator, September 27, 2019.

One ship I served on, the *London Citizen*, was a six-hatch tween decker, meaning that it had a second deck for holding cargo between the main deck on top and the hold space below. The *Citizen* also had a midship superstructure. One time in the Port of Maputo in Mozambique (formerly known as Lourenço Marques) we were assigned the task of loading a full cargo of 40 ft-long steel I-beams. This proved to be very difficult, because our cargo holds and spaces were not configured to carry long steel beams. The number one cargo hold and tween decks could not be used, because the hatch was too small.

Even with a steel cargo, we filled all of the available space where the beams would fit. In number four, the beams had to be loaded on an angle to pass through the hatch opening. The Zulu dockers used greased boards and muscle to lever the beams inside the tween decks. It was an arduous task. The cargo took three weeks to load. When we arrived in Detroit, the discharge lasted just two days. Removing the I-beams was swift compared to the human sweat required to stow them.

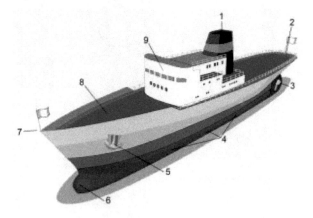

1. funnel, 2. stern, 3. propeller, 4. hull plating, 5. anchors, 6. bulbous bow, 7. bow, 8. deck, 9. superstructure. Public Domain.

Ship Measurements

The size of a ship is quoted in terms of gross tonnage, displacement, deadweight, length, beam, draft and air-draft.

Gross tonnage is calculated by measuring a ship's volume (from keel to funnel, to the outside of the hull framing) and applying a mathematical formula. It is often misunderstood, because it refers to the ship's volume, not weight. It can be calculated in different ways: there is a gross tonnage, 'gt'; a net tonnage, 'nt'; the Suez Canal also has its own versions of gt and nt that are calculated differently.

Displacement is the ship's weight and its cargo, i.e., the total weight of the water that the ship is displacing. Light displacement is the weight of the ship with no cargo. Load line displacement is the weight of ship and cargo to its maximum allowed draft. Deadweight is the total weight of cargo, fuel and stores that a ship can carry.

Length can be the length overall, 'LOA', or it can be the length between perpendiculars measured at the waterline, 'LBP'. Beam is the maximum width of a ship at its widest point; this is important for safe entry into canals and locks or suitability for cargo operations involving shore-crane outreach.

Draft is the vertical distance from the bottom of the ship's hull to the waterline. The draft is read at six points on the hull: the bow, midships and the stern on each side. By taking visual readings of the six points, the ship can calculate the displacement from tables provided by the shipbuilder. After allowing for the ship's light displacement, fuel and stores, the ship or a marine surveyor can then calculate the amount of cargo on board.

Air-draft is the vertical distance from the highest point on the ship to the waterline. This is important to ensure that a ship has sufficient clearance to pass under bridges.

During the winter season, the Gulf of St Lawrence in Canada is frozen with sea ice. Navigation can be severely impaired when a ship becomes stuck in an ice pack under pressure from the prevailing wind. When I was chief mate on the *Ontario Power*, we routinely traded between Sydney, Nova Scotia and Sept-Îles, Québec during the winter. The *Ontario Power* was not ice-strengthened and had a low propulsion speed of about 10 knots. We frequently spent days stuck in the ice pack and had to wait for a change in the wind direction or an ice breaker to free us. `

On the other hand, when I was the chief mate on the *Phosphore Conveyor*, ice class 1 with 19,000 shaft horsepower, the ice in the Gulf was no match for us. On our voyages to Sept-Îles, we often acted as the volunteer ice breaker: we would pass close to ships that were stuck, and they would break free and fall in behind us. We would often collect half a dozen ships, and they would steam along in our wake as we forged a path through the ice.

I served as chief mate on the *Canadian Transport*, which was contracted to load ilmenite (titanium-iron alloy) ore at the Québec port of Havre-St-Pierre. The *Canadian Transport* had been built at the Kure shipyard in Japan by Daniel K Ludwig, with a very wide beam at 116 ft. The loading conveyor at Havre-St-Pierre had been designed to load standard Great Lakes vessels, which had a beam of just 76 ft. The challenge was how to load the maximum cargo of ore with a loading conveyor that could not reach the center of the ship. The trajectory of the ilmenite as it fell from the conveyor caused the cargo to fall 3 ft off the center. The ship was listing to one side due to the imbalance.

The solution was to use the offshore upper wing ballast tanks to provide a counterbalance. Although the water ballast reduced the amount of cargo, the amount of ballast needed was minor due to the position of the ballast tank and the effective leverage that it provided. As chief mate, I developed the system, and the *Canadian Transport* worked efficiently on this route for two years of her life.

The relationship between ship construction and the voyage is one of a seafarer's many challenges. Ships all share common attributes concerning their construction. They also have uniquenesses that set them apart, however, because they were designed to perform a specific trade or operate under particular conditions. Seafarers are familiar with the common platform. They adapt their skills and knowledge to manage the unique features that define the ship they are assigned to operate across a global platform safely.

3

STEEL, PAINT AND RUST

———❧———

Chipping Away

SS *United States* in Philadelphia, August 2020. CC BY-SA 4.0.

Corrosion is the natural enemy of ships built of steel plates.

When the plates are rolled to thickness from a steel slab, they begin life with a thin layer of blue-black 'mill scale', iron oxides which initially protect the steel from atmospheric corrosion. Mill scale is short-lived protection, however; it flakes off easily as the steel starts rusting, and that sheer blue-black gives way to many shades of brown.

For longer-term protection, the steel needs painting, and the layer of mill scale has to be removed by abrasive blasting or by pickling the steel in a bath of acid. If the paint goes on without first removing the mill scale, it will just flake off along with it.

Putting Steel Plates Together

The components of a ship, including the hull and the decks, are all fabricated from steel plates. During construction in a shipyard, they are built in large modules that are lifted into place and assembled by welding.

Before World War II, rivets connected the plates. Riveting was a labor-intensive process: plates had to be overlapped and holes had to be drilled between each plate. A hot rivet was placed into the hole with a cap that held it in place on one end and a round bar slightly smaller than the hole in diameter on the other end. The cap side was held in place while the other end was hammered and shaped to form the opposite cap. As the rivet cooled, it shrank, and this pulled the two plates together.

Rivets can still be seen on the *Queen Mary* in Long Beach harbor. The *Queen Mary* sailed on her maiden voyage in 1936, and her hull is entirely made up of overlapping plates held together by rivets. If you get a chance to see this, remember that every one of those ten million rivets was placed by hand and hammered in.

Rivets on the bow of the RMS *Queen Mary*. David Reid.

During World War II, the Emergency Shipbuilding Program in the U.S. pioneered the welding of steel plates to speed up the work of rapidly constructing merchant ships as a response to the sinking of merchant ships by German U-boats. Between 1941 and 1945, 2,710 'Liberty ships' were launched. Liberty ships were general cargo ships with a cargo-carrying capacity of 9000 tons. The tanker version was known as the T2, and the Sun Shipyard built the most common version in Philadelphia with a turbo-electric propulsion system. Liberty and T2s shared a common problem, though: cracks in their hulls, attributed to poor welding techniques and a type of steel plate that was brittle under cold temperatures. Additional belts of steel were installed to provide extra support.

My first ship was a bulk carrier that had been converted from a tanker. The hull had been welded originally, but the entire length was fitted with a belt of heavy steel plate that was riveted to the original deck. At the time, I just thought that was normal, and it was only years later that I recognized that this had been added during the conversion to provide longitudinal strength to the original hull and compensate for the bulk carrier's large hatch openings.

Corroding Ships

Salt water is particularly corrosive to steel. Any crack or tiny opening in the paintwork that allows moisture to make contact with steel gives it a foothold. The steel begins to corrode as it oxidizes, and the reddish-brown rust forms as the oxygen in the water and the iron in the steel combine. Onboard a ship, this deterioration is called 'wastage' and can disintegrate entire sections into dust if undetected. Enclosed spaces like ballast tanks are a problem because the steel is exposed to moist air conditions whenever the tanks are empty. Once, on an ore carrier called the *Finnamore Meadow*, I was making a routine inspection of a ballast tank. When I turned my flashlight, I was shocked to see large sections of the steel supports had simply disappeared!

Every classification society requires ships to undertake special surveys at five-year intervals. The surveys at 15 and 20 years become more intensive. The surveyor looks for wastage of steel using non-destructive methods such as ultrasound. When steel is found to be heavily wasted, it has to be replaced before the ship is allowed to continue trading. Sometimes the extent of the corrosion is such that the cost of repair exceeds the commercial value of the ship; in such cases, the ship is destined for the breaker's yard.

Ocean-going ships, much like horses, 'age' about three

times as fast as humans: a 15-year-old ship can be viewed, like a 45-year-old human, as middle-aged, whereas a 25-year-old ship would be a senior citizen at 75. Consider, then, the devastating loss of the *El Faro* in 2015. The *El Faro* was built in 1975 and was 40 years old at the time of the loss: in human terms, it was about as viable as a 120-year-old.

In Canada, many ships trade on the freshwater Great Lakes system, where they can enjoy much longer life spans without the effects of saltwater corrosion. The US-flag laker *J.B. Ford* operated for 112 years before being retired to the breaker's yard.

J. B. Ford at the scrapyard. CC BY-SA 4.0.

Fighting Rust

Maintenance at sea can begin only once the decks have been washed and the gear has been stowed. Areas exhibiting signs of rust are prepared for painting with chipping hammers, scrapers and wire brushes. The wooden-handled chipping hammer has a double-chisel-shaped head and is used to repeatedly strike the steel to remove the shards of flaking rust. The area is then scraped and brushed before receiving a coat of primer.

As a navigating cadet on my first and second ships, the work program often included many days of chipping and scraping followed by painting. You become attached to your chipping hammer: I remember mine was issued to me by the chief mate. After a few days of use, you find just the right place to hold its handle so that the hammer balances nicely as you swing it for each blow, settling into a rhythmic cycle that lasts for hours and hours... I went to sea to become a navigator, but in that first year, I knew more about chipping and painting than reading a chart or learning the rules of the road.

Chipping is a repetitive physical activity that requires minimal thought. I found that I could pass the time chipping away while thinking about other things. When chipping on deck plates, we would sit on small wooden stools and steadily chip away at vast areas of plates encrusted with thick layers of rust. It was a delight to reveal the real steel beneath, heavily pitted though it was from the effects of oxidization. On a few occasions, my chipping hammer went further than planned, and a hole opened up: a clear indication that the section was heavily wasted. These holes had to be reported to the chief mate, and an engineer would temporarily repair them by welding a doubling plate over the top.

For the mariner, corrosion is the enemy within. Fortunately, there have also been advances in shipbuilding to keep it at bay. Plates have the mill scale removed before welding. Modules are built indoors for better paintwork quality. Paint systems have advanced, providing more excellent adhesion and resistance to wear. Coatings inside ballast tanks and enclosed spaces prevent corrosion from diminishing the unseen parts of the ship. Despite all these improvements, however, rust is still ever-present and will find places where paint has been damaged.

One of the most hazardous places for rust is the interior of wire ropes, particularly the wire ropes that hold ships' gangways and lifeboats. Several incidents have occurred because the wire cables had not been lubricated and corrosion had eaten away at the wire cable. As a chief mate on the Canadian self-unloader *Ontario Power*, I was making a routine check of the cables that held our 250 ft unloading boom suspended during discharge. To my horror, I found numerous broken wire strands, indicating that we had a severe problem. Changing the wire was an immense and complex task, but I felt much better when the new cable was in place and given a good dose of protective lubricant. When the old cable was removed, we found the inner core heavily corroded.

In my early days at sea, I never understood why I had to spend so much of my time chipping away. Looking back, I now appreciate what this taught me about rust and the damage that it can do. Rust is an ever-present latent defect that increases exponentially as every ship ages. It deserves respect.

4

SPEED, FUEL AND ENGINES

―∾∾―

At a Rate of Knots

Thomas Walker, inventor of the 'log' measures of speed and distance at sea. CC BY-SA 4.0.

For those of us who have been at sea, the unit 'mile' can mean two different things: the statute mile, used on land, corresponds to 5280 ft, or 1609 m; while the nautical mile, used by seafarers, is longer at 6080 ft, or 1852 m. Why do seafarers use a different mile? The National Oceanic and Atmospheric Administration (NOAA) provide the following explanation:

Nautical miles are used to measure the distance traveled through the water. A nautical mile is slightly longer than a mile on land, equaling 1.1508 land-measured (or statute) miles. The nautical mile is based on the Earth's longitude and latitude coordinates, with one nautical mile equaling one minute of latitude.

But why use a different measurement system for marine navigation? Using latitude and longitude coordinates is more practical for long-distance travel, where the curvature of the Earth becomes a factor in accurate measurement. Nautical charts use latitude and longitude, so it's far easier for mariners to measure distance with nautical miles. Air and space travel also use latitude and longitude for navigation and nautical miles to measure distance.[1]

Because ships measure their distance traveled in different miles than other vehicles, they also use a different unit to measure their speed: one nautical mile per hour, called a 'knot'. The term 'knot' comes from the knots on the 'common log', a 17th-century measuring device. A piece of wood attached to the ship by rope would be dropped off the stern, and the sailors would watch the rope run out as the ship moved away. There would be knots tied at set intervals along the rope, and when a certain amount of time had elapsed the sailors would pull the wood back in and count the knots.

Precisely measuring speed on a ship is now possible thanks to the GPS satellite system. Before the GPS, speed was estimated based on engine speed adjusted for local currents and weather. When the ship's position was known, either from electronic navigation aids or celestial observation, the distance traveled and the average speed could be calculated.

As the second mate on the British cargo ship *London Statesman* on trans-Pacific voyages, my regular tool of choice for measuring speed was the Walker Cherub log. The Walker Cherub log was a brass impeller attached by a plaited rope to a meter mounted on the ship's rail off the stern quarter.

The impeller would rotate as it was pulled through the sea. This action twisted the rope, which in turn caused the gears inside the meter to rotate. The meter was read daily, and this simple device indicated the ship's speed through the water. Allowances still needed to be made for other factors, but it was helpful when cloudy conditions prevented celestial observation. The downside was that the brass impellers were often taken by sharks, who mistook them for fish, leaving the rope trailing along. We carried spare impellers, but once they were used, the log was out of action.

Ship Speeds

When ships are built and chartered, the ship's capability is described as a service speed of knots consuming a given amount of fuel under normal weather conditions.

Ships are not fast compared to other modes of transport. A typical bulk carrier or tanker may have a service speed of 13 knots, which translates to about the usual speed restriction when driving a car through a school zone. Imagine if that speed was the average speed of travel for driving a car. Presuming no adverse currents or weather to contend with, a ship travelling at 13 knots can cover a distance of 312 nautical miles every 24 hours. A truck driver would comfortably achieve the same distance in 5 hours.

Some ships can have higher speeds, but they have to consume more fuel. Shipowners and charterers, therefore, look to balance the economics of their daily running costs against the cost of fuel. They decide on a speed that optimizes their commercial economics. This type of calculation has given rise to what is known as 'slow-steaming' or 'eco-speed'. In a high-demand cycle, where ships are in short supply, a high speed makes sense; conversely, when shipping is experiencing a low demand cycle, there is no urgency, and the economics favor saving fuel costs with a slower speed.

Left: SS *Sirius*, first Blue Riband holder (8 knots, 1838). Right: SS *United States*, current holder (34.5 knots, 1952). Public Domain.

Cruise ships and ferries typically have the higher speed to manage scheduling and can achieve speeds of up to 25 knots. For military and tactical reasons, naval ships have still higher speeds of up to 35 knots. The highest speed crossing the Atlantic by a passenger liner (unofficially honored as the 'Blue Riband') was set all the way back in 1956 by the SS *United States* during her trials. Formally, she still holds the title and was comparable to a naval ship.

Container ships have similar propulsion capability to the modern cruise ship, with speeds of 20 knots or better. When the American shipping company Sealand built its SL-7 class of container ships in 1971, they were capable of 33 knots. When fuel prices escalated in 1973, however, the economics made them unprofitable, and the US Navy acquired them in 1981 for military deployment.

Speed at sea can be severely affected by weather and sea conditions, and on trans-ocean voyages, the weather can bring ships to a virtual standstill. In 2021, several ultra-large container ships experienced loss of containers from their decks while battling through extreme weather. It is not unusual for ships to report several days of delay in their estimated time of arrival. When the weather and sea conditions combine to limit progress, the ship often has to alter course or slow down to avoid damage to the ship and its cargo.

Each ship will also handle weather and sea conditions differently depending on its size and type of construction. Ships that have a lot of deck cargo and superstructure are heavily affected by wind. The effects of ocean currents and weather significantly change the difference between speed through the water and speed over the ground.

During World War II, merchant ships sailed across the North Atlantic in convoys protected by navy escorts. However, the speed of the whole convoy was governed by the slowest ship, so they traveled at speeds of 10 knots, managing only 240 miles per day. Convoys were most vulnerable to German submarine attack in the zone between coast lines, because they could not receive air cover from land. This zone was called the 'Black Pit' and took up to five days to travel through.

Convoy Routes in the
Atlantic Ocean during 1941.
Public Domain.

Fuel and Engines

When a voyage is planned, the speed and fuel
consumption must be carefully calculated, especially when
the ship is loading a full cargo. The primary purpose is to
earn freight, which means maximizing the payload. Extra
fuel can reduce the cargo carried, but ships need a safety
margin of fuel or 'bunkers' in case of delays due to bad
weather. Typically, on a trans-ocean voyage planned for 25
days, a four-day margin would be factored into the plan.

On the *London Statesman*, while crossing the Pacific, we
encountered severe weather for more than three weeks and
at times were 'hove to', just keeping the ship headed into

the weather while making no progress. For days on end, we encountered extremely heavy pitching and rolling. The swells of the sea were so deep that when the ship pitched forward, the propeller came clear of the water and caused the main engine to race as resistance was lost. The main engine speed had to be reduced to a minimum. The ship's galley had difficulty preparing meals under such conditions.

After the first week of this battle with the Pacific, everyone on board was sleep-deprived and stressed. As we neared the Japanese coast, the engineers reported that we were almost out of heavy fuel oil for the main engine. Our reserve margin had been fully used. For the last day of our voyage, the main engine and the generators would be using our limited supply of marine diesel oil. When we dropped anchor in Tokyo Bay, the engineers reported zero fuel in all the tanks. Fortunately, the Tokyo shipping agent had a bunker barge standing by, ready to fill us up.

Technical faults can also impact the speed at sea. Ships have power systems that drive the propeller, most commonly in the form of a slow-speed marine diesel engine that is coupled directly to the propeller. To reverse or go astern, the engine first has to come to a stop, have its control systems switched and then be restarted in the opposite rotation.

Most ships have a single marine diesel engine for propulsion, so if there is a fault, then the engine is stopped, and the problem has to be fixed. Ships' engineers can replace most of the major components such as pistons and cylinder liners. Repairs might take anywhere from a few minutes to 36 hours. It is never an easy task, however, if the ship is pitching and rolling. If a repair cannot be made, the master will need to summon an ocean-going tug to return the ship to port.

Stern of the *El Faro* on the seafloor. Taken by Cable Underwater Recovery Vehicle (CURV) aboard the Military Sealift Command Fleet ocean tug USNS Apache (T-ATF 172). Public Domain.

The Liberian-flag *Phosphore Conveyor*, where I served as chief mate, was an ice-class Panamax bulk carrier with twin diesel engines driving through a gearbox to a single propeller. Mid-Atlantic, one of the engines suffered a problem with contaminated lubricating oil in the crankcase and was damaged. Shortly after that, the second engine failed because the design had a common sump serving both engines. The *Phosphore Conveyor* was stranded mid-ocean and had to be towed to Hamburg for repairs at the shipyard. The rebuilding of both engines took more than nine months. Problems with lubricating oil contributed to the loss of the *El Faro* when her steam turbines shut down due to low oil levels in the sump, and low oil levels were also the reason for the total loss of power on the cruise ship *Viking Sky* in 2019.

For seafarers, the main engine is the beating heart within every ship. The steady vibration represents comfort; silence means danger. Even at slow speed, if the ship is moving itself it has control. When momentum is lost completely, the ship is left vulnerable and exposed.

NOTES

1. NOAA, 2021. *Ocean Facts: What is the difference between a nautical mile and a knot?* https://oceanservice.noaa.gov/facts/nautical-mile-knot.html. Accessed 2021.

5

NAVIGATION

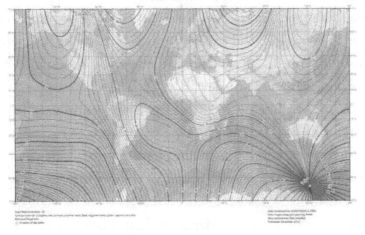

1° Course Change

US/UK World Magnetic Model - Epoch 2015.0
Main Field Declination (D)

Magnetic Horizontal Declination or Variation in 2015. US
National Oceanic and Atmospheric Association, Public Domain.

Seafarers have carefully worked to evolve their techniques and plot the safest routes possible for their ships over thousands of years. For all that evolution, though, and even the incredible technological advances of the last 50 years, the fundamentals remain the same: from Viking *knarrs* to ultra-large container ships, celestial observations to satellite signals, navigation has always come down to the two critical elements of direction and time.

Direction

Historically, mariners have determined which way they were going by the compass. It may surprise many to know that the Safety of Lives at Sea (SOLAS) Convention requires all ships to carry a magnetic compass, but it is still an important backup if the gyrocompass and other electronic aids are somehow disabled. In its simplest form, the compass requires no electricity, relying only on the earth's magnetic field to keep its needle pointing magnetic north. Mariners can then refine the needle's information by applying variation and deviation.

A straight line on a flat Mercator projection is called a 'rhumb line'. The actual shortest route between two points, which appears as a straight line along the surface of a globe, is called a 'great circle' route. Everyone that has flown internationally has experienced the great circle navigation used by airlines. On a Mercator chart, however, the great circle appears as a curve, and it typically requires the ship to steer a different course every 24 hours. Maintaining the right course is critical: over the course of a day, even a 1° error results in a 5 mile difference.

The route planned may not always be the shortest distance. The great circle route from Tokyo to Los Angeles, for example, passes close to the Aleutian Islands near Alaska, through some of the heaviest winter weather and seas. When a ship's course is planned, everything has to be taken into consideration, including the weather, prevailing currents, known hazards, the ship's condition, draft and the limitations of load line zones. The paramount consideration is planning the safest route for delivering the best result. Mariners may evaluate the weather and choose to plot a rhumb line course, a great circle course, or a hybrid course that uses both in different sections of the voyage.

For many years, the paper chart was a key tool for planning routes. Some ships' chart rooms carried libraries of 3000 charts, covering every part of the world. Nautical charts are produced and sold by two principal organizations: the British Admiralty Hydrographic Office and the US Hydrographic Office. According to the Admiralty, 90% of ships trading internationally rely on their charts.[1] The Admiralty has a library of 3500 paper charts and now also offers a digital library of 14,000 charts for the Electronic Chart Display and Information System (ECDIS), which displays the ship's position overlaid on a digital chart.

Chart room table and chart drawers on the RRS *Discovery*. David Reid.

An extensive portfolio of paper charts requires constant manual correction. It consumes many man-hours, but it is critical to safety, because the new corrections might include reports of a hazard like a change of depth or a new position for a buoy. The second mate is responsible for managing the chart portfolio.

When ships relied on mail via the post, the chart corrections came in the form of booklets called 'notices to mariners'. At first, notices to mariners were simply lists of changes. Later, the changes came with tracing overlays that made the process faster. After each correction, the second mate would initial and date the chart to show the most recent edit. Nowadays digital charts have streamlined the correction process and integrated the chart with electronic positioning devices. ECDIS also integrates satellite positioning and the chart onto a single digital platform, where paper charts required the watchkeeper to plot the ship's position manually by pencil and ruler.

During my time as a second mate, the delays in ship's mail caused constant headaches for me. Charts had to be corrected sequentially in chronological order, so when a mail packet went astray, I had to wait for the missing weekly notices to arrive. Once they were received, many hours of work in the chart room followed: charts were removed from the drawers, all the changes were made on them, and each correction was noted in the lower-left corner. The notices to mariners were also a reciprocal process, relying on reports from mariners in the case of a deviation from the chart. In 1973, I reported a buoy that was in the wrong position in the St Lawrence River; some weeks later, I was delighted to find my report included in the weekly notices to mariners. That was my favorite chart correction of all time.

Time

Besides the direction of travel, mariners must know the time, which, when in motion around the globe, is inseparable from position. The mathematics of celestial navigation for measuring latitude are elementary: a sextant can be used at noon to take a measurement of the sun's angle at its zenith, called 'a sight'. On a cloudy and overcast day when the sun was not visible, the celestial navigator would have to estimate the ship's position and mark it on the chart with the initials DR for 'dead reckoning'. My initials are DR, so, as a junior navigator, I received many jokes about positions that I plotted on the chart.

Longitude is harder to get than latitude, because the sun's angle does not change as a ship moves from east to west. An accurate chronometer (marine clock) is necessary, but for a long time, navigators didn't have one on board a ship. Instead, sailing ships would 'parallel navigate', working up or down a coastline until they reached the desired latitude, then sailing east or west along that parallel until they reached the opposite coast. This only worked because they could measure their latitude at noon each day.

Twin binnacle magnetic compass on the RRS *Discovery*. David Reid.

In 1714, following several tragic maritime disasters attributed to poor navigation, the British Government established the Longitude Act, which promised incentives to anyone who could solve the problem. John Harrison, a carpenter by trade, devoted his entire life to designing and building a maritime clock. Capt. James Cook used Harrison's K1 chronometer on his second and third expeditions. Capt. James Bligh of HMS *Bounty* used K2, and, after his crew mutinied, Fletcher Christian who took command kept using it.[2]

The traditional chronometer is manually wound, so, like the magnetic compass, it required no electricity. Manual winding, like chart correction, was the responsibility of the second mate. It relied on taking sights of the sun's precise height in the sky, which was hard to distinguish at noon, so the sights for longitude were usually taken about three hours before noon on British ships.

For these sights, it was necessary to have a person at the chronometer inside the chart room to record the time of each sight. The sun rises rapidly in the morning, so the time of the angle measurement was critical for accuracy. The navigator standing outside on the bridge wing would make a distinct sound or shout a word like "time!" to let the recorder know when to note the time of the sight.

Taking morning sights was often a group exercise, with the master, second mate and third mate all taking sights and calculating position lines. Needless to say, as a junior officer, you hoped that your result would come close to your seniors'. On my first time at the chronometer, I waited nervously; the old man (master) always went first. I heard something that sounded like a dog bark, so I quickly noted the time. Apparently the dog bark was the old man's signature.

The rise of satellite navigation, not only in ships but in our cars and our pockets, would suggest that the role of the sextant and the taking of sights would be redundant. However, there are good reasons to retain the ability to use these basic navigation skills. The United States Navy has resumed training in celestial navigation and the sextant as a contingency if the GPS satellite system is disabled. Merchant ships also retain the sextant, and shipping companies require that their watchkeepers practice the use of celestial navigation.

No Batteries Required

With these three basic tools – a magnetic compass, a chronometer and a sextant – any ship can be navigated without electricity or satellites. While serving in the Canadian merchant marine, I experienced the importance of keeping my skills up. My ship, the *Ontario Power*, relied on Omega, a system that received broadcast radio signals and calculated the ship's position, but one time it failed mid-Atlantic. As chief mate with deep-sea experience, I was the only navigator on board with a sextant. With no Omega to guide us, I went back to basics and took morning and noon sights. My Canadian colleagues watched in amazement as I took my sights and calculated the ship's position: I had turned into a living history lesson.

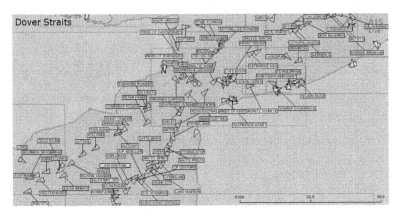

AIS display of the English Channel/la Manche and the Dover
Straits. Public Domain.

Since 2002, IMO-SOLAS has made it mandatory for all
ships to be fitted with Automatic Identification System
(AIS). AIS enables the automatic exchange of information
between ships and shore receiving stations such as Vessel
Traffic Services (VTS). AIS transformed the shipping
industry forward in one quantum leap. Before, a ship could
only know the name of another ship by communicating via
VHF radio or by signaling via the Aldis lamp in morse code.
Today, any pilot station or port authority can observe all
the ships in their immediate area on a screen. Each ship
transmits a set of key data providing the name, position,
course, speed, etc. Onboard a ship, AIS is integrated into
ECDIS and is a component of the integrated navigation
system. AIS is now also viewable via many commercial
internet ship information tracking systems. Thanks to
satellite AIS receivers, we now can view the 50,000
merchant ships moving around the world's oceans in real
time.

Today's navigator works on a bridge packed with integrated systems that aid the task of keeping the ship safe. However, when ships suffer technical problems or when satellite-based systems are interrupted, the navigator can fall back and rely upon the magnetic compass, the chronometer and sextant; no batteries required.

NOTES

1. Admiralty Maritime Data Solutions. *About Us.* https://www.admiralty.co.uk/ukho/About-Us. Accessed 2021.

2. For more on John Harrison, see Dava Sobel, 1995. *Longitude: The True Story of a Lone Genius Who Solved the Greatest Scientific Problem of His Time.* New York: Bloomsbury.

6

ROPES AND MOORING

The Monkey's Fist

A sailor tosses a heaving line to pass a mooring line to a handler on shore. CC BY-SA 3.0.

The heaving line is a lightweight throwing line used to establish connection between ships and docks. It is made from 30 m of 6 mm rope. Typically, two members of the mooring party will have heaving lines ready to throw towards the dock as the ship approaches the berth. Throwing to the linesmen waiting on the dock is a critical moment during the mooring of any ship. The ship is steadily moving ever closer to the waiting berth, aided by a tug or multiple tugs. The pilot on the bridge uses the ship's engines and bow thruster, if fitted, to maintain a measured rate of approach. Berthing is typically made on a slight angle to the dock, so the mooring party on the forecastle will be the first ones to dispatch a heaving line.

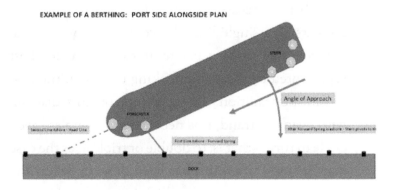

EXAMPLE OF A BERTHING: PORT SIDE ALONGSIDE PLAN

Diagram by David Reid.

Throwing a heaving line requires practice and strength worthy of an Olympic sport. The individual who sets up to make the throw has many eyes focused on them as they hold the line in their hands and look to the waiting hands ashore. Throwing too early may mean the line misses the dock and falls into the water. Throwing too late means a delayed deployment of the first line ashore. To give the throw momentum, a 'monkey's fist' is attached at the end.

If you own one of those display boxes containing a selection of knots, the monkey's fist is one of the many knots you will find. The *Ashley Book of Knots* describes it as follows:

> The monkey's fist is a spherical covering with six surface parts presenting a regular over-one-and-under-one weave. This weave is commonly doubled or tripled to present an appearance that superficially resembles a Turk's-head. Like the Turk's-head, the knot is tied with a single strand, but here the

resemblance ceases. The Turk's-head diagram consists of a single line; the common monkey's fist diagram has three separate lines, which are best represented by three interlocking circles, in the best Ballantine tradition. To tie a knot on this diagram with a single strand, it is necessary to complete each circle in turn—that is, to double or triple it, as the case may be—and when this has been done to deflect the strand into another circle which is completed in turn before commencing the third and last circle.[1]

Monkey's Fist. CC BY-SA 3.0.

For even more weight, there used to be a bad practice of adding a steel nut inside the monkey's fist, but this has since been prohibited as unsafe by the Code of Safe Working Practices for Merchant Seamen. The monkey's fist can, however, be dipped into white or orange paint; while technically meant to make the line more visible at night, the paint also soaks into the fibers to give some additional weight.

Mooring

On the forecastle and the bridge, everyone watches as the monkey's fist goes into orbit with the heaving line snaking behind. There is a sigh of relief when the monkey's fist lands on the dock and the heaving line is firmly gripped by the line handlers ashore. The other end of the heaving line is already attached to the eye of the first mooring rope to go ashore.

The mooring lines are the head line, stern line, breast line and the forward and aft spring lines. The first line is usually the forward spring line, which leads towards the ship's center, aft from the forecastle and forward from the stern. Getting the first spring line ashore can significantly assist the pilot in bringing the rest of the ship alongside gently, because it acts as both a brake and a pivot point to swing the stern into line with the dock.

EXAMPLE OF A MOORING PLAN 3:1:1. [3 HEAD/STERN LINES, BREAST LINE AND SPRING]

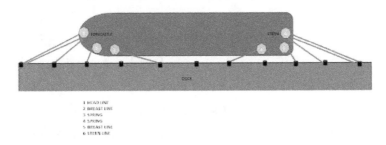

1 HEAD LINE
2 BREAST LINE
3 SPRING
4 SPRING
5 BREAST LINE
6 STERN LINE

Diagram by David Reid.

The eye of the mooring rope is passed through the fairlead

rollers, and the rest of the line is hand-fed by the mooring crew once the line handlers are ready to pull it ashore. When the line handlers place the eye of the mooring line on the mooring bollard on the dock, they pass the eye through the eye of other ropes on the bollard. This clever trick allows any rope to be released as needed.

Linesmen placing a mooring line on a bollard in Rotterdam. Picture by Danny Cornelissen, courtesy of Portpictures.nl.

The mooring lines are made from synthetic fibers like polypropylene and nylon. Before the advent of synthetic fibers, they were made from the natural fibre of the abacá plant, more commonly known as Manila hemp. Synthetic ropes have the advantage of being easier to handle because they are lighter and do not absorb water, so that they float where Manila ropes would sink. Synthetic ropes also have very different characteristics under stress, however, and are prone to severe snapback when they break.

In 1971, during a port call at the port of Rouen in France, the *Overseas Adventurer* was at a river berth, port side alongside. The Seine River in France experiences the phenomenon of tidal bore or, as it is known in Rouen, *le mascaret*: a mini-tsunami of water that rushes upstream in rivers prone to significant tidal variations. Before the tidal bore arrived, we ceased cargo operations, raised our gangway and set extra moorings.

As a navigating cadet, I was assisting the second mate at the stern. Our synthetic spring line parted with a loud 'snap!' as the ship surged astern in the tidal bore's wake. I watched the mooring line go vertically upwards and land with a thud on the dock, in the opposite direction to when it was running from our ship. If anything, or anyone, had been in its way, they would have been seriously harmed.

Seine River tidal bore at Caudebec-en-Caux.
Raymond Huon. Courtesy of Sequana-
Normandie, CC by attribution.

When the eye of the synthetic rope is secured ashore, the mooring crew can pass the rope around the drum of the winch, and the rope can be made tight. The next step is to pass the rope onto the mooring bitts on the forecastle or stern. This has to be done while not losing the tension on the mooring rope, so a rope stopper is used. The rope stopper is attached with a shackle to the bitts.

Shipboard bitts on the RV *Thomas G. Thompson*. By Joe Mabel, CC BY-SA 3.0.

The rope stopper is wrapped around the mooring rope and the end held by a crew member. Then the rope on the drum can be slacked off, and the loose part of the mooring rope can be wrapped around the bitts, usually in a figure-eight pattern. Once secured, the rope stopper can be released. This procedure is performed for every mooring rope that is sent ashore. Depending on the circumstances, that can be at least five ropes at each end of the ship, sometimes more.

It takes time to throw the heaving lines, pass the mooring ropes, retrieve the heaving lines (the linesmen throw them back onboard), heave each rope tight, set a rope stopper and transfer to the bitts, but this operation has to take place no matter the weather conditions or time of day or night.

When it's below freezing with a severe wind chill at three in the morning, it takes longer than on a warm sunny day.

Some ships use mooring wires instead of synthetic ropes, and the ships that ply the Great Lakes and St Lawrence River use wire cables from self-tensioning winches that allow the operator to set the winch on automatic tension. Wire ropes can only be used with dedicated winch drums, because they are difficult to secure over mooring bitts. They still require a heaving line to enable the wire rope to be passed ashore, but with the weight of the wire cable, they can only be dispatched once the ship is close to the dock.

On the bridge, as a ship makes its final approach to the dock, two key moments are noted in the bell book and ship's logbook: first line ashore and all fast fore and aft. The final task for the mooring crew is to set the rat guards over each of the mooring ropes. Rat guards are compulsory in all ports and function bi-directionally. On my first ship, the *London Prestige*, one of our daily routines as navigating cadets was to check all the rat traps in the store lockers and to provide the captured rats with a proper burial at sea.

Tying Things Up

After leaving port, all the ropes need to be removed from the forecastle and stored below in the rope locker. This is to protect the ropes from prolonged exposure to ultraviolet light and to keep them safe during heavy weather. The ropes are returned above deck before arrival at port. Ropes and wires that are drum-mounted are covered with canvas protectors and well secured.

When a ship leaves the berth, the first step is to 'single up fore and aft', taking in all the lines except for the two springs, one headline and one stern line. Then the stern lines are released and winched on board. The order of this sequence is critically important because it ensures that no mooring lines are floating near the propeller. The bridge will wait for the all-clear message from the stern before making any engine movements. The usual routine when departing a berth is to use the forward spring to pivot the ship's stern away from the dock. Once the pivot is underway, the last headline is taken on board, and as the ship moves astern and away from the dock, the final spring line is taken onboard.

There have been some technological advances to simplify mooring in the St Lawrence Seaway. Some of the locks have been fitted with vacuum pads that are integrated into a sliding mechanism at the side of the lock. The ship enters the lock, and the vacuum pads adhere to the ship's hull and hold the ship in place while the lock water level is raised or lowered.

This technology has allowed automated control of the locks since no linesmen are required.

If the ship has to wait at the approach wall, however, it is still necessary to tie up. That means landing two crewmembers ashore using a landing boom unique to the St Lawrence Seaway. A seafarer wearing a lifejacket is seated on a wooden board suspended by a rope to the arm of the landing boom. The boom is swung outboard, and once the seafarer is vertically over the dock, they are slowly lowered down. All of this takes place while the ship is gradually moving towards the dock. As soon as the two seafarers are landed, they take the heaving lines and receive the first mooring lines.

Hands-free mooring system in the Eisenhower Lock. Courtesy of Great Lakes Seaway Partnership.

The art of mooring a ship to the dock is timeless. Ships have changed in many ways, but even the most sophisticated ships afloat still need a seafarer to throw a heaving line to line handlers ashore. Heaving lines are pulled so that the mooring ropes can snake their way to a bollard on the dock. Onboard, the mooring ropes may be on a dedicated winch, or they may require to be pulled tight by wrapping around the drum end of the winch. One constant has remained steadfast; the monkey's fist is always the first one to get ashore.

The Heaving Line. Arthur Briscoe, 1926. National Gallery of Art. CCO.

NOTES

1. Clifford Ashley, 1944. *The Ashley Book of Knots: Every Practical Knot -- What It Looks Like, Who Uses It, Where It Comes From, and How to Tie It.* New York: Doubleday, Doran, & Co.

7

THE GANGWAY

Umbilical from Ship to Shore

Crew setting up a gangway. David Reid.

The ship's gangway, or 'accommodation ladder', as it is properly known, has remained essentially the same in the past 50 years. Yet this humble and seemingly forgotten aspect of nautical design performs an extremely important function. Access via the gangway is the primary access for all shore personnel, including vendors, chandlers, agents, regulatory officials and large numbers of longshore workers. As chaplains and ship visitors, we are also frequent gangway users.

Many shore personnel are not conversant with the fact that, when a gangway is being used in a suspended mode, the interface is dynamic. The ship can move and quickly change the relationship between the dock and the foot of the gangway. Even when gangways are landed, they are still prone to sudden movement.

Gangway Safety

If you underestimate it, a gangway can be dangerous from the bottom to the top. You should never step onto the lower platform at the bottom without having a good handhold on the railings. Many accidents have taken place at the lower platform when the lower platform has not been fully horizontal or not fully secured, or simply when someone has slipped.

At a major terminal in the Port of Philadelphia, an experienced marine surveyor stepped onto the lower platform of a ship's gangway and immediately fell between the ship and the dock. The pin securing the lower platform had not been secure. Fortunately for the surveyor, the gangway net had been properly rigged, so he landed in the net and not in the hypothermia-inducing cold water of the

Delaware River. The surveyor was a master mariner and well versed in ships gangways. He routinely boarded ships as part of his work. This example illustrates two things: that even the most experienced can become complacent, and that the gangway represents a risk that ship visitors need to respect.

Ten key aspects of gangway safety stand out to me as things everyone using gangways needs to be mindful about:

1. Gangways are narrow. They are a one-way system, so always give right of way to those coming up. Wait at the top for clear passage before starting down.

2. When walking up a gangway, you should always have one hand free to hold the handrail and ideally both. Never carry anything which prevents you from holding on.

3. On larger ships, the length of the gangway and the height of the climb may be very significant. Be prepared to pause during the climb to avoid being stressed.

4. Be extra careful during inclement weather when the treads of the steps may be slippery or icy. Gangway steps are designed with a curved profile so that they function at both shallow and steep angles.

Gangway. Courtesy of the Seamen's Church
Institute flickr.

5. Every gangway is required to have a safety net
   that extends 2 m forward and aft of the gangway
   itself. The net is to avoid anyone falling into the
   gap between the ship and the dock. This is
   particularly relevant at the foot of the gangway,
   where people must transition between the dock
   and the lower platform.

6. In some cases, the gangway may be rigged from
   the main deck or under a working cargo area.
   Avoid using the gangway when cranes are
   working overhead.

7. Many ships now post signs stating the maximum
   number of persons permitted on the gangway at
   any one time. Larger ships and longer gangways
   mean that their safe working load can be
   exceeded with too many persons using them at
   once.

8. Be mindful of 'jury-rigged' things, like planks being used to create a bridge between the dock and the lower platform of the gangway.

9. When ships are working cargo and pumping ballast, the gangway is in constant need of adjustment. This may also be due to large tidal changes in some ports. If the lower platform of the gangway is not aligned with the dock, stop and request the duty officer or deck watch person to adjust the gangway.

10. In some ports, when ships are heavily loaded and the dock has a high wall, the main gangway will be hard to deploy, so you may see other access ladders deployed. In some cases, terminals may deploy a shore gangway for a limited period of time. Often these are rigged over the ship's bulwarks or railings, so there will be a second set of steps to be traversed in order to reach the deck. It is always safer to descend these second steps backwards, using three points of contact at all times.

What Not to Do

The Nautical Institute in London will celebrate its 50th anniversary in 2022. The Institute has been a strong advocate of safety at sea, encouraging members to share details of accidents near misses. The Institute's monthly magazine, Seaways, includes a report from the Maritime

Accident Report System (MARS). All of the ships, people and locations in reports are anonymous; the sole purpose is to share what happened and why. MARS is also maintained as a searchable database[1] that all of its members can access. In writing this chapter, I did a quick search of that database and found six gangway accidents profiled in recent years.

In over 50 years in the maritime industry, I have rigged gangways as a cadet, supervised them as a deck officer and been responsible for their maintenance as a chief officer. As a stevedore manager and terminal operator, I cannot remember how many different gangway scenarios I have experienced; all I can tell you is that they are many and varied.

In more recent years, serving as a chaplain in the Port of Philadelphia I have experienced yet more gangway moments. One that serves as an example was during my visit to a 13,000 teu container ship that was lightly loaded and therefore had a very high freeboard. I was leaving the ship after spending an hour listening to members of the crew share their experiences of their brand-new ship. As I arrived at the head of the gangway to hand back my shipboard security pass, I observed a large group gathering on the dock, perhaps 20 or more. I headed down the very long and steep gangway and stepped back on to the dock. Recognizing some faces in the group, I realized that it was an official visit, including the local press, to welcome the new ship to Philadelphia. As I stood on the dock waiting for the terminal bus to take me back to the gate, I observed the officials and journalists follow each other up the gangway.

Unfortunately, they had not read the sign that limited the number of persons on the gangway to five. Because it was a very large container ship with a very long gangway, the group just kept marching up, adding more people until the entire group filled the gangway. Fortunately, the ship was brand new, and the gangway was suspended on its cables, all in good condition. They were all lucky enough to make it safely to the main deck without incident, and I hope on their way back down someone reminded them of the importance of reading safety signs.

When using any gangway to board or disembark a ship, remain situationally aware. *Stop.* Observe the gangway and its environment *before* you put your foot on it. *Always keep one hand for you and one for the ship.*

NOTES

1. https://www.nautinst.org/resource-library/mars/mars-reports.html

8

HEAVY WEATHER

Expected and Respected

The prevailing weather dominates life at sea and directly impacts both the ship's progress and the living conditions for the seafarers on board.

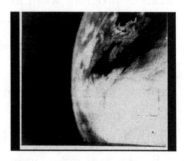

The first television image of Earth from space, taken in 1960 by the TIROS-1 weather satellite. NASA, Public Domain.

Before NASA launched the weather satellite TIROS-1 in April 1960, merchant ships themselves would serve as weather stations, reporting the weather they observed to meteorologists. In return, the meteorologists compiled the data received and determined the location of weather systems. The weather reports could then be sent in a coded form that the navigating officer could then decipher.

Meteorology

The first maritime weather forecasts were released in 1861 as a response to tragedy. Two years earlier in 1859, an unexpected storm had sunk 133 ships and killed around 800 people off the western coasts of Scotland and Wales. The storm was named the 'Royal Charter Storm' after its largest victim, the steam clipper ship *Royal Charter*, which was lost with around 450 of its passengers and crew. By 1911, the UK Meteorological ('Met') Office was routinely issuing marine weather forecasts. In the United States, the first marine weather program was initiated by the United States Army Signal Corps around 1873 in New Orleans, but was transferred to the United States Weather Bureau in 1904. Like the UK Met Office, the Weather Bureau collected weather observations from merchant ships. During World War II, stationary weather ships were stationed in both the North Atlantic and North Pacific.

By the mid-1980s, weather ships had been phased out. Satellite observations have radically changed both the collection of data and the accuracy of forecasts. Weather charts are updated and generated with computer software, making them more accurate and much easier to understand.

One legacy measurement that has remained in place is the Beaufort scale for wind and sea conditions. The scale was invented in 1805 by Francis Beaufort, an Irish hydrographer and Royal Navy officer. The scale specifies 13 categories from 0 (calm conditions) to 12 (hurricane conditions), each with their own wind speeds and wave heights.

Sir Francis Beaufort. Royal Museums Greenwich, Public Domain.

The Beaufort scale became the standard for sea observations aboard all Royal Navy ships in 1830 and was adopted by the 1st Meteorological Conference in Brussels in 1853.

The simplicity of the Beaufort scale is that it communicates conditions, observed or forecasted, with one simple number. There may be some interpretation as to whether conditions are, say, 6 or 7, but there is no difficulty understanding the difference between 6 and 8. The scale remains the fundamental metric for marine weather worldwide.

Pitch and Roll

Like everything else that floats in the water, ships follow

the Archimedes Principle, which dates back to its namesake's famous 'Eureka!' bath in 246 BC. Archimedes determined that any object totally or partially immersed in the water is buoyed up by the water with a force equal to its own weight and displaces an amount of water equal to it in weight.

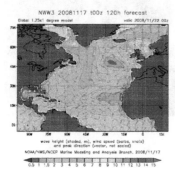

NOAA Wavewatch III 120-hour wind and wave forecast for the North Atlantic. NOAA, Public Domain.

This principle explains why ships refer to their 'tons of displacement': the ship's weight determines the weight of water it displaces and the amount of force supporting it. The volume of water that that weight reflects can be greater or less based on the water's density, so the ship rises and sinks as the space it takes up in the water changes. A ship floating in salt water is more buoyant; when the ship enters a river with fresh water, the draft increases.

Buoyancy also means that ships are prone to movement as they encounter the waves and swells of the great oceans. These movements are affected by the ship's stability: when the ship's center of gravity is deeper in the water, the force of the water on either side working to bring the ship back to its normal upright position is greater and works faster. In these conditions, seafarers refer to the ship as being 'stiff'.

While stiff condition is generally positive, it does mean you can experience fast cycles of rolling and pitching. The experience feels like an amusement park ride. The converse condition, 'tender', is more dangerous, though, because the forces to

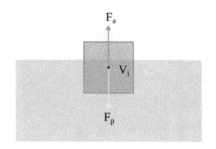

Weight (Fp) and buoyancy (Fa) must be equal in force. CC BY-SA 4.0.

return the ship upright are reduced and the rolling cycle is much longer. In a long rolling cycle, the ship moves side to side in a wide arc: if it rolls 20° in one direction, you can expect it to roll 20° in the other direction as it corrects itself, so the actual arc will be a whopping 40°. Everything must be secured as any loose items will be on the move, and it becomes hard to move safely around the ship. All of this is especially dramatic when you are on the bridge, far above the ship's center of gravity.

Besides stability, a ship's size, displacement and angle with the waves all affect the way it pitches and rolls. For example, when a ship is head-on into the waves, the pitching may result in the bow being lifted out of the water and slamming back down. The resulting severe vibration throughout the whole ship is known as 'pounding'. In some cases, the stern is also lifted out of the water, causing the propeller to break the surface, and that causes the engine to race. In such cases, the engine speed has to be reduced to avoid damaging the propeller shaft. Conditions may become so severe that the best course of action is to hold course into the weather and 'hove-to', keeping just enough propeller speed to maintain direction but not enough to actually go anywhere. Sometimes, when the course of the ship is at an angle to the direction of the waves, ships will pitch and roll simultaneously.

SS *Waratah*, Blue Anchor Line.
Public Domain.

Rolling at tender stability can be an especially dangerous combination. When I attended the Plymouth School of Navigation, our lecturer Graham Danton[1] told us the story of how in July 1909, the SS *Waratah*, a passenger and cargo liner, was making her return voyage from Australia to Europe by way of South Africa when she disappeared between Durban and Cape Town. 211 passengers and crew were lost, and no trace of the *Waratah* was ever found.

The ocean area adjacent to the South African Coast is known for its abnormal 'freak' waves of extreme heights, and the marine inquiry believed that the *Waratah* was loaded tender to make the ship roll gently for the comfort of the passengers. Danton speculated that the *Waratah* could have easily fallen prey to 'synchronous rolling', the phenomenon of the ship and the waves rolling in time together, 'resonating' and building on each other. Once caught in synchronous rolling, the ship could have heeled, rolled over and become unable to return upright. I never forgot that lecture and firmly believe that Danton's teaching saved me and my crewmates' lives just a year later.

It was the summer of 1973, and the *London Statesman* had just sailed from Durban following the same route as the *Waratah*. We were loaded with raw sugar bound for Canada. The winds were moderate, but there was a heavy swell on our beam and we were rolling about 20° as I took my afternoon watch. As the afternoon wore on, our course kept us beam on to the prevailing Indian Ocean swell, and I took up my position near the steering stand to observe the clinometer needle.

As we rolled, and I watched the brass needle swing, in the back of my mind I realized that each period of roll was a degree or two greater than the previous one. We were now passing 25°. In those minutes, I could hear Danton's lecture on synchronous rolling in my mind. The rolling increased to 30°, and I realized that I needed to act. There was no time to call the master to seek advice.

I made my way to the autopilot and switched to manual steering as the roll rose to 35° in each direction. As we came out of the roll, I changed our course by 25°, hoping to change our period of rolling and remove the possibility of resonance. I held my breath as the bow began to respond to the rudder and breathed again as we broke free of the swell and the rolling eased and changed to a pitch and roll. I kept a different course for the next few hours until it was safe to resume.

I will never know how close we came to disaster that watch. What I did realize then and have remembered ever since, is that our lives can be altered very quickly if we are not alert to what is going on around us.

The ship's motion increases the daily stress level for seafarers. It complicates simple tasks and can disrupt sleep and rest. Each cycle of severe shocks and vibrations affects seafarers' mental state. During extreme weather, the cook may not operate the galley, and meals may be limited to sandwiches and whatever the cook can manage through the gyrations. As the extreme weather goes on, sometimes for many days, the whole crew can suffer from a form of traumatic stress and fatigue from using more energy to maintain balance and having to hold onto things constantly.

The experience can be exacerbated when there is a problem with cargo or stores breaking loose and remedial action needs to be taken. During one trans-Pacific voyage, our ship had to jettison part of the deck cargo that had broken free. Even more troubling was the night that our starboard lifeboat broke free from its securing and was at risk of further damage. Fortunately, we managed to re-secure, but situations like this made me very mindful of the unlimited power of the ocean.

When we visit ships in port, perhaps we do not always appreciate the securing latches and high sills on doorways we need to step through. We also might wonder why the chairs are attached to the deck and the messroom tables all have raised edges. The seafarers well understand this. When the ship is at sea, however, the latches keep the door watertight and the high sills help prevent seawater from flooding in. The reality of life at sea is that heavy weather has to be both expected and respected.

NOTES

1. Author of the 1962 classic *The Theory and Practice of Seamanship*. London: Routledge & Kegan Paul.

9

FIRE ONBOARD

~~~

Disasters at Sea

Smoke rising from a fire on two
Tanzanian-flagged Turkish ships, *Maestro* and
Kandy in the Kerch Strait near the Black Sea.
CC Attribution SA 4.0.

Fire on a ship is seafarers' worst nightmare and one that
comes true all too often. There have been many fires on

84

container ships. In May 2021, the global news networks reported dramatic footage of the container ship *X-Press Pearl* burning and sinking off the coast of Sri Lanka. In March 2018, the ultra-large container ship *Maersk Honam* caught fire off the coast of Oman. According to Allianz, the German insurance company, the fire took five days to fight, caused hundreds of millions of dollars in damage and killed five of its 27 crew.[1]

How Fires Start

A fire on a ship can have three primary sources: the engine room, the accommodation, or the cargo. Engine room fires are usually the result of either electrical faults or pipes carrying flammable liquids bursting. The engine room can be evacuated, sealed and flooded with carbon dioxide to suppress a fire. Engine rooms and machinery spaces are also closely monitored, making it possible to take prompt action.

It is critical to address an engine room fire quickly, because once the main engine shuts down, the ship loses propulsion and becomes vulnerable in heavy weather or confined waters. If the generators also shut down, the ship then becomes reliant on its backup emergency generator. The emergency generator is located in a separate space from the main engine room, but if the cabling or control systems are damaged, then electrical power can also be compromised. This further exacerbates the danger, because lighting and navigation systems, including communications, will be affected.

The accommodation space comprises all of the living and

social areas onboard the ship and includes the most common sources of fire: the galley and the cabin. Cabin fires, most often caused by a cigarette, can occur both at sea and in port and can spread quickly through the combustible materials like bedding and clothes found nearby. They must be extinguished using hand-held extinguishers or with water from a fire hose.

Cargo fires vary based on the type of cargo and the ship. On container ships, it is impossible for those on board to tell whether what is inside a container is packed safely or not. Other cargoes are inherently flammable, and extreme precautions must be taken with those. Whether in dry forms like coal or in liquid forms like oil and liquified gas, all hydrocarbons have to be controlled by keeping them in inert spaces. On a tanker, the most significant risk actually used to be when the tanks were empty, because the mixture of air and volatile compounds provided the perfect ingredients for an explosion.

In a period of just three weeks in 1969, three very large crude carriers, the *Mactra*, *Marpessa* and *King Haakon VII*, all experienced major explosions, and the *Marpessa* sank. The cause of the explosions was attributed to static electricity discharge during tank cleaning. The solution was mandatory inert gas systems to eliminate the oxygen inside the tanks. These safer gas systems extracted nitrogen from the ship's exhaust, providing an organic solution that made tankers safer.

Large car carriers have also suffered cargo fires. Fires spread rapidly between cars packed very close together, so that when one vehicle has a problem, it spreads like a virus. In 2020, at the Port of Jacksonville, the car carrier *Hoegh Xiamen* was completely destroyed in a major fire. It had loaded a cargo of used cars destined for West Africa.

King Haakon VII after the explosion.
terjefossen.com.

Firefighting

Besides the work assignments they are trained and employed to do on the deck, engine, or galley, all seafarers have to be firefighters. When fire alarms are triggered onboard, the entire crew transforms itself into a coordinated fire-fighting unit. At sea, there is no emergency number to summon firefighters: you are alone. Even in port, however, shore-side firefighters are not always familiar with ships, so the first response and the incident command are still the master and crew's responsibility.

Fire drills are conducted regularly onboard: fire pumps are started, hoses run out, and the portable breathing apparatus is tested. During port state control inspections, the coast guard will routinely require a full fire drill and will closely observe the equipment, deployment and state of readiness shown by each crew member.

I experienced a cabin fire onboard the *Canadian Transport* while berthed at the Port of Sorel in Québec. The *Canadian Transport* was the largest ship under the Canadian flag at the time. I was in the mess room taking my lunch with the chief engineer when one of the galley messmen rushed in and shouted "Fire!" The chief engineer dashed to the engine room to get the fire pump started, and I, as chief mate, headed straight for the scene.

I found the problem on the port side, in one of the crew cabins. Thick smoke was pouring out. I had summoned the duty mate and the deck crew, and they ran out the fire hose and connected it. There was water pressure: the engineer's fire pump started.

I approached the alleyway adjacent to the cabin with the nozzle set to 'mist' to cool down the structure. We opened the adjacent cabins, pulled out the mattresses and flammable materials and soaked the adjacent bulkheads. Finally, once the surrounding area was safe, we opened the cabin door and extinguished the fire.

A mattress had caught fire, and as best we could determine, it was the result of a cigarette. This all happened very quickly: no more than ten minutes. The duty officer had notified the stevedores, and the Sorel fire department had been summoned, but the fire was out by the time they arrived.

Ship Disablement and Evacuation

In 2013, a fire broke out in the engine room of the passenger ship *Carnival Triumph*. It was extinguished, and everyone was safe, but the damage to the engine room resulted in the loss of power and propulsion. There were delays with the backup emergency generators, and services had to stop. The *Carnival Triumph*'s passengers endured some pretty unusual conditions onboard.

Taking to the ship's lifeboats and rafts is a critical decision, made only by the master after evaluating all the available options. In heavy weather and rough seas, launching lifeboats may itself be dangerous. If a fire cannot be extinguished, however, and the ship becomes disabled or at risk of sinking, it may be necessary to abandon the ship.

An example of this type of situation occurred in the winter of 2019, when the cruise ship *Viking Sky* lost all power and propulsion off the coast of Norway. It began drifting towards the rocky coastline, and the master contacted the Norwegian Coast Guard to evacuate the passengers by air as a safety precaution. The ship's engineers were fortunately able to restart the main engine and restore power with 100 m to spare, but it was a near miss: despite a massive rescue operation with six helicopters, only 100 of the 915 passengers had been airlifted. The *Viking Sky* is a reminder of how, when a ship is disabled, the challenge of evacuation during inclement weather has its inherent limits and risks.

In 1970, I was serving as a junior officer on a tanker, the *Overseas Adventurer*. One day, during a brief port call in London, my father took the opportunity to visit my ship for Sunday lunch. As we were stepping out onto the main deck to say our goodbyes, I turned around to see him with a cigar and his favorite Zippo lighter! I shouted and managed to stop him before he flicked. The *Overseas Adventurer* was loading oil and venting the tanks, so any flame would have been extremely dangerous. He was very embarrassed, but no harm was done. That incident has always reminded me of how dramatic a simple mistake can be on a ship.

NOTES

1. Allianz, 2018. *Expert Risk Articles*. "Industry's struggle with container ship fires continues". https://www.agcs.allianz.com/news-and-insights/expert-risk-articles/container-ship-fires.html. Accessed 2021.

10

LIFEBOATS

Last Resort

Lifeboat in the modern style, mounted on a slide
for easy launch. David Reid.

Before the innovation of a designated lifeboat, the ship's workboats had to serve a dual purpose of ferrying people ashore at an anchorage and helping in an emergency. The first shore-based lifeboat is believed to have been designed and built in 1790 by Henry Greathead in South Shields, near Newcastle-upon-Tyne in northeastern England. It was intended as a rescue boat that could go out to assist anyone in distress near the coast and had a self-righting feature should it be overturned in heavy seas. The concept of designated lifeboats on ships came with the age of steam propulsion. Brunel's SS *Great Britain*, launched in 1839, carried three lifeboats on each side.

From 1839 to 1914, the carrying of lifeboats was guided by the 1849 Passenger's Act and the subsequent 1854 Act. These regulations were all based on tonnage and not the number of passengers carried, and anything beyond the statutory minimum was at the sole discretion of the shipowner. White Star Line, the owner of the *Titanic*, had fitted more lifeboats than they were legally required to carry, but not enough for all onboard.

When the *Titanic* collided with an iceberg 20 minutes before midnight on April 14, 1912, the world became aware of the importance of the humble lifeboat. Many of the passengers and crew could not escape the sinking ship and drowned because it was not a requirement to carry sufficient lifeboats for all. The subsequent inquiry and investigation led to the introduction of new safety regulations. The International Convention for the Safety of Life at Sea (SOLAS), came into effect in 1914 with an essential requirement that every ship carry lifeboat capacity sufficient for all onboard.

While such a requirement may seem obvious now, at the inquiry, numerous experts testified that it was not necessary. The wisdom put forward was that a few lifeboats could be used to ferry people to other rescue ships, and therefore lifeboats to carry everyone at once were superfluous. Another argument was that so many lifeboats would upset the aesthetic look of these great liners, which after all were designed to reflect grandeur and style.

Using a Lifeboat

At the time of the *Titanic*, the method to launch wooden lifeboats was cumbersome and labor-intensive, requiring a well-trained crew both in the lifeboat and on deck to lower them with rope falls. It was a far drop from the deck to the water level, and failure to control the speed of descent could mean losing the lifeboat. Seafarers at each end had to work in harmony to ensure that the forward and aft rope falls were kept level.

During my time at sea, one of the routine jobs for the navigating cadets was checking the lifeboat provisions. The open-style lifeboats carried water tanks under the seating benches, and these would be refreshed on a regular basis. Storage lockers contained tins of hard biscuits and jars of barley sugar. We would check the condition and count the tins and jars. Every time that I did this, I found myself wondering what it would be like to be with 50 people in a lifeboat passing around biscuits and barley sugar to eat.

The equipment onboard included fishing line and hooks with the assumption that we might catch our food. Our lifeboats had a mast together with a sail and oars, and the starboard lifeboat had a diesel engine which rarely started during a drill. The port lifeboat had no engine, but it did have a manual propulsion system operated by pushing and pulling handles from the seats of the boat. The prayer was "If we have to launch, let it be the starboard lifeboat and let the engineers be able to get the diesel engine started."

More than one hundred years on from the *Titanic*, lifeboat design has improved. Most ships now have fully enclosed motor-powered lifeboats rather than the open design with oars or manual crank-driven propellers. Merchant ships have for many years been required to carry a lifeboat on each side of the ship with capacity in each lifeboat for the full crew, because if the ship has listed, only the lifeboat with a clear vertical drop to the waterline will be able to swing over the side.

The latest innovation for merchant ships is the single, stern-launched lifeboat. It uses methodology developed for evacuating offshore oil platforms, where time is of the essence and nobody needs to remain on deck to manage the launch. These lifeboats are mounted on an angled ramp, and the crew simply strap themselves in and then release the lifeboat to freefall down the ramp and into the sea: a quick, one-way trip! This type of lifeboat launch was shown in the Tom Hanks movie, *Captain Phillips*, the real story about the *Maersk Alabama* being captured by Somali pirates on April

8, 2009. The lifeboat from the *Maersk Alabama* is now on display at the Navy Seal Museum in Fort Pierce, Florida.

Worth the Risk

Most people have some limited knowledge of what a lifeboat can and cannot do. Anyone that has taken a cruise will have been through a lifeboat drill and asked to put on their lifejacket and present themselves at the designated muster station. As a former seafarer, I am not a fan of the modern mega-liners; I shudder to think of what will happen when a mega-liner has to evacuate the full complement of thousands of people at sea, especially now that the ratio of crew to passengers on liners is even lower than in the Golden Age. We know that in incidents like the *Costa Concordia* the evacuation process did not go well, and, even though the ship did not sink and was very close to shore, 32 people lost their lives.

Indeed, very few maritime disasters have been salvaged by lifeboats. When merchant ships sink, the circumstances are often too severe or happen too quickly for the lifeboats to be launched. This was the case when the *Marine Electric* was lost in 1983; only three of the crew survived, and they sought refuge in an inflatable life-raft after the ship sank in the Atlantic. All of the crew were lost from the *El Faro* in 2015 during Hurricane Joaquim; she had been built in 1975, and her lifeboats remained the classic open-style lifeboat, the shipowner never having upgraded them to a modern design. The only wreckage found of the British-flag ore carrier *Derbyshire* was one of her lifeboats, drifting empty in the

Pacific. The loss of the *Edmund Fitzgerald* in 1975 on Lake Superior was similar; there was no time to abandon ship. In a more recent ore carrier loss, the *Stellar Daisy*, only two seafarers survived, and they took refuge in one of the ship's inflatable life-rafts.

As a chaplain, when I visit merchant ships, I observe the ship's lifeboat and remember my own experiences of launching a lifeboat into the sea while anchored off the Port of Monrovia. I was serving as the third officer on an ore carrier called the *Finnamore Meadow*, and there was a queue of ships at anchor waiting their turn to load Liberian iron ore. Most of the ships were under the British flag, and we had communicated with another ore carrier about swapping our reel-to-reel movies (in the '70s, well before the age of VHS or DVD, each ship carried a film projector with three full-length feature movies supplied in a metal container). We decided that we could creatively combine a lifeboat drill with a film exchange. We were several miles offshore, and there was a light breeze and a low swell. Good conditions, I thought.

I learned that day how different the sea can look when viewed from a lifeboat. I was the officer in charge of the drill. I saw firsthand how fragile we were as we descended the boat deck suspended by two wire cables. As we approached the water 50 ft below, I issued instructions to the seamen stationed forward and aft to make ready to release the hooks. As we came close to the sea, a low swell lifted us up for a few seconds and then fell away, causing a sharp shudder as the wire falls took the strain of the boat's weight.

We hit the water, and the hooks were released; however, we now were rising and falling with the swell while still tethered to the ship by a rope called a 'painter'. We had successfully released the hooks and wire falls, but they now were dancing around our heads, and we had to duck and weave to avoid being struck.

I powered up the Lister diesel engine and we motored ahead to clear the swinging wire falls. The painter was released and brought onboard and I turned to make way towards the other ship. The vantage point from the lifeboat was very different than from the deck of our ship. The low swell seemed much higher and the light breeze felt stronger.

We made it to the other ship, exchanged our films and returned. The task of recovering a lifeboat is a more significant challenge than the launch, because you have to time the moment to attach the wire falls and hold them in place while the boat bounces up and down in the swell. The hoist motors on the articulated arms that receive the lifeboats, called 'davits', are slow, and there is a significant risk of injury in those minutes while you dangle in the no man's land between being afloat and on deck.

Sadly, there have been many cases of seafarers losing their lives or being seriously injured during lifeboat drills in port, even under calm conditions. The IMO now recommends doing the exercise first by lowering and recovering the lifeboat without any persons in the boat and after that with only the minimum to operate the lifeboat; prudent advice, but not exactly a vote of confidence in the system's usefulness for emergencies.

Lifeboats with capacity for all are a statutory requirement on ships. For seafarers, however, they are a last resort that will not help if the weather is severe or if the event plays out suddenly. Lifeboat drills remain a fixture, but the newer, stern-launched lifeboats cannot be drilled, and with conventional side-launched lifeboats there is less appetite for practice launches given the risks. Instead, the lifeboat sits on its launch ramp or hanging from its davits, waiting for the moment of release; a moment that every seafarer knows signals a last-ditch resort.

11

STRESS

A Maritime Constant

North Pacific storm waves as seen from the NOAA
M/V *Noble Star*, winter of 1989. NOAA. Public
Domain.

For those who have never worked onboard a merchant ship,
it may be difficult to comprehend the stress that affects the

daily life of a seafarer over their entire stay at sea. While some stressors are easier to deal with than others, and some have an easier time dealing with them, all carry risks to mental and physical wellbeing.

These considerations are very important in work as a port chaplain. When I meet seafarers, I am looking for signs of stress. I try to connect them with friends and family for support and try to provide some of that support myself. Seafarers' missions and organizations around the world are very focused on their welfare. The International Seafarer Welfare and Assistance Network (ISWAN), based in South London, provides 24/7/365 assistance to seafarers via a hotline connection.

Stress needs to be considered holistically. The human body does not differentiate mental health from physical; stress affects the mind, body and spirit of every seafarer. To understand the wellbeing of a seafarer we cannot consider mental health in isolation.

Throughout my eight years at sea, the majority of my experiences were positive, but I did serve with people who were stressed by the environment and clearly suffered various states of anxiety and depression. I am aware of two disappearances of senior officers under circumstances attributed to them taking their lives. Suicide is the extreme case, but the life of a seafarer is affected by all of the factors which affect everyone plus the uniqueness of their life at sea. We need to be aware and mindful of the stress and be ready to help.

Stressors Onboard

One of the jobs that I feared most during my time at sea was entering enclosed spaces, especially cofferdams, double-bottoms and the mud box below the chain lockers. Even as I write this now, I can feel my body tensing into fight-or-flight mode and my level of anxiety rising as I remember having to clean out the mud box below the chain lockers.[1] Access was through an oval manhole that required you to wriggle through into the cramped and muddy 2 ft-high space under the pile of anchor chain. Even though it has been more than 50 years since I did that work, it feels as if it was yesterday.

My anxiety about being trapped in a confined space is my personal traumatic stress. For others, there are other situations which create anxiety or depression. As a cadet, I experienced numerous times when I had close calls involving enclosed or confined spaces. Perhaps my fear saved me from danger. It did not save me from anxiety or stress.

There is one constant that remains a focal point of stress for all seafarers, and that is the impact of heavy weather. In port, ships are upright and static as they lay peacefully alongside the berth. At sea, however, during a force 12 storm, swells may tower more than 15 m or more in height. The ship will be moving, vibrating, shuddering and shaking as it combats the immense energy of the ocean. These conditions may last for days and weeks during major transatlantic crossings; it is not unusual for large and modern ships to lose days in their expected arrival time because their transit speed drops to the bare minimum to maintain steerage.

In 1973, while I was serving as the second officer on the *London Statesman*, we were loading a cargo of sugar in the Port of Durban. At the adjacent berth, I observed first-hand the bow of the damaged British cargo liner *Bencruachan*. Just before arriving in Durban, the *Bencruachan* had encountered a freak wave during the night. This had caused the entire forward section of her bow to drop by a massive 20 ft, pleating her hull's steel plates like a kilt. They were lucky to have not gone down. The sight of steel folded by the power of the sea made me realize how powerful the ocean can be.[2]

When ships sail through extreme weather, the master and mates have to pay close attention to how the conditions affect the ship. There are times when the ship is taking a beating and straining under the constant impact of heavy seas and swells. It feels something like what I imagine a boxer feels receiving blow after blow from his opponent. Unlike the boxing ring, however, there is no time provided to recover between rounds. The art of seamanship is knowing when to take preemptive action before something bad happens.

Once I was sailing to Philadelphia on the Canadian bulk carrier *Ontario Power* with a hold full of gypsum. It was November, and the first of the Atlantic storms were making themselves known. As we passed east of Nantucket, we were pitching and rolling heavily, shuddering after each punch. The *Power* was definitely uncomfortable. On the bridge, it was technically my watch, but the master was there sitting in the pilot chair. This was his first voyage in command, and we knew each other well. As more punches came, I wondered why he did not want to act. I became concerned because the *Ontario Power* was a self-unloader with conveyor tunnels below the cargo holds running the ship's entire length. Even with watertight doors, I knew that we had a higher risk of sinking than a standard bulk carrier.

I decided that it was time to act. I stood next to the master and quietly suggested to him that we alter the course for a while to ease the strain. His reaction was immediate, as if he had been waiting for the prompt. He told me, "Good idea!" I altered our course to port, and immediately the shuddering ended. The *Ontario Power* relaxed back into a gentle rhythm. Within six hours, we were able to resume our course for Philadelphia. Our minor deviation had added an hour to our voyage, but we arrived safely.

Providing Relief

As a chaplain, I do my best to assess the level of stress: Are the seafarers tired? What type of mood are they in? Do they have a positive or negative expression? On a recent visit, I met a third engineer who clearly needed to get ashore. He was tense and worried. He asked if I could take him to a shop where he could send money home. Recognizing that this man was apparently under stress, I told him that he could come with me and that I would bring him back. This news brought the first sign of a positive expression, and as we left the vessel and proceeded ashore, I wondered why he needed to wire money home.

Typically, seafarer's wages are paid by direct deposit into their bank accounts, and this means that their families have funds available to pay their mortgages and meet their ordinary expenses. Seafarers will take a cash draw at a port to get money for shopping, but otherwise, a merchant ship is in effect a cashless society. Once signed onto a ship, there is nothing to buy, so seafarers only need to retrieve their wallet during the few times that they will venture ashore.

Many seafarers may experience periods of several months before a suitable shore leave opportunity presents itself. Often, the reduced time in port, logistics and security challenges all present formidable obstacles to get ashore. For seafarers working six-on, six-off watches, choosing to get ashore means giving up rest time or taking on the added stress of a double-watch later.

So why did the third engineer need to wire money home, and why was this so urgent? The rest of the story revealed itself as we drove along in the mission van, newly provided by a grant from the ITF Seafarers' Trust. As a chaplain, I simply ask questions: "Tell me about your family back home." As we drove along the highway, my passenger began to talk about his family and his young wife who had just given birth to his daughter, a daughter that he had only seen on Skype. The conversation continued in great detail about his life as a seafarer and the different shipping companies that he had worked for. It was during the dialogue that he revealed the real issue that was at the root of his stress: the company had been paying his wages late, and his wife and family were in desperate need of funds because the direct deposit of wages had not been paid.

Here, we also see why communications for seafarers is so important. Today almost all seafarers have smartphones. I had just delivered two wifi hotspots onboard his ship, enabling the seafarers to connect to the internet for free. (The wifi hotspots are provided in part by a grant from the North American Maritime Ministry Association (NAMMA) in conjunction with the ITF Seafarers' Trust). The third engineer was upbeat about the wifi onboard, because he would be able to let his wife know that the money was on its way. On our return trip he was in a much better mood. As we parted at the foot of the gangway, I could see in his face that a heavy burden had been lifted.

In the 21st century, one might ask what the role of mission in the modern shipping industry is. The answer is that we are on the frontline of the wellbeing of seafarers. An active presence onboard the ship does make a difference, as do internet connectivity and transport ashore. Seafarers will experience stress in the everyday rhythm of their voyage. In a place of safety, we will hear about the latest hurricane that threatens the coast, or the one that has now departed.

In our shore-based lives, we will rarely be conscious of the many merchant ships that are at sea doing their best to navigate through storm systems, or what being onboard those ships in heavy weather does to the health of a seafarer. Imagine the stress that a seafarer experiences when they are not able to connect with their family for several weeks. For most of us today, the loss of service for just a few hours would cause unbelievable stress on its own, not to mention sleep deprivation, loneliness and an intense workload. We can, therefore, appreciate how important our seafarer missions are and why they are an integral part of a healthy shipping industry. For seafarers, welfare and listening ears are not just nice to have; they are necessities.

NOTES

1. See the chapter 'Ship Construction'.
2. Not long after I had my own close call in those very waters. For that story, see the chapter 'Heavy Weather'.

PART II

THE WORLD OF SHIPPING

12

THE SUPPLY CHAIN
AND CARGO

Floating Conveyor

In his classic of economics, *The Wealth of Nations*, Adam Smith stressed the importance of specialized production and international trade, stipulating that:

Adam Smith bust in the Adam Smith Theatre in Kirkcaldy. CC BY -SA 3.0.

1. trading relationships between nations are driven by supply and demand,
2. surplus resources in one country are needed by others and
3. bilateral trading arrangements may focus on raw materials flowing in one direction and finished goods in the other.

Global trade has been steadily developing since when Smith was writing in the 18th century, but these basic principles of exchange remain in many ways the same even today.

The business of the world shipping fleet is to transport the materials that flow between nations. Today this fleet is some 50,000 merchant ships strong, employing 1.5 million seafarers to keep the 'floating conveyor' in motion.

Seaborne trade represents 90% of world trade. The United Nations Conference of Trade and Development

(UNCTAD)'s 2017 statistics put seaborne trade at 10.7 billion tons and revealed steady growth over the past 25 years.[1] In 2019, 11.1 billion tons moved between nations: 7.9 billion tons (two thirds) was dry cargo, with a balance was crude oil and other tanker trades. Asia leads the world in seaborne trade.

Several vital raw materials form the basis of the seaborne trade. The 'main bulks' category, which makes up 3.3 billion tons traded, includes iron ore (about 45%), coal (40%) and grain (15%). The 0.8 billion tons of the 'break bulk' sector are equally distributed between steel and forest products.

Tons carried isn't a proper measure of shipping in and of itself, however. To understand the scope of global trade, we need to factor in the distance those tons are moved. This metric of 'ton-miles' shows the real flow of materials around the world. From the UNCTAD data, we can see that the ton-miles needed to run the global conveyor has actually increased by 50% in the past ten years. This takes either more ships, higher velocity, or a combination of both.

Iron Ore: a Case Study in Raw Material

I spent the second half of my maritime career working in the supply chain of the steel industry. The making of steel requires three primary materials: iron, coal and limestone. In the UNCTAD data, iron ore makes up a significant portion of sea trade at over 1.5 billion tons. The coal used for steel is a particular type, known as 'metallurgical' coal, which is used as a feedstock to produce coke, the fuel that 'cooks the rocks'.

Limestone is needed in the mix as a catalyst to separate the iron ore. During the 'cooking' or smelting, the non-iron elements in the ore attach to the limestone, forming a lighter liquid known as 'blast furnace slag', while the heavy iron flows to the bottom of the furnace. Although the slag is a by-product, it too is traded by sea in bulk after cooling and granulation. It is used for the production of cement and in road construction.

After iron ore is open-mined from natural deposits, it is usually transported unprocessed to sea terminals. Most unprocessed iron ore is shipped with a natural Fe (iron) content of 62%, so a ship loading 300,000 tons of primary iron ore is carrying only 186,000 tons of actual iron. The balance is made up of other elements and moisture. Moisture has to be monitored and certified by the shippers to ensure that the ore is not subject to the dangers of liquefaction. Too much moisture can result in the ore being liable to shift within the ship's cargo holds.

The supply chain must move 5 tons of iron ore to produce 3 tons of pure iron. At first glance, it would seem illogical to consume vast amounts of ton-miles to transport the non-iron constituents. Looking closer, however, shows what is moving and why. The global system of mining and steelmaking has evolved to drive down the cost of shipping iron ore over long distances by using ultra-large ore carriers that can load up to 300,000 tons. The sea terminals that receive unprocessed ore are also very large to accommodate them.

Reducing primary iron ore to a higher iron content is

also possible, and in some supply chains, the preference is to ship pelletized iron ore with higher iron content. The challenge when dealing with iron, however, is that it is not stable and naturally attracts oxygen to form iron oxides. So, while it is technically feasible to produce iron briquettes, it is not so easy to transport them.

Unlike iron, semi-finished steel is moved in large volumes very efficiently. In Brazil, a country with vast iron ore reserves, the mining company Vale has had steel plants established on the coast to transform iron ore all the way into semi-finished steel ready for export. Over the past 40 years, several such large steel plants have been purpose-built in Brazil, each with support from Vale. California Steel Industries (CSI) is a finished steel products rolling mill in southern California. When CSI started operations in the mid-80s, it depended on shipping from the first dedicated semi-finished steel plant in Brazil, Companhia Siderúrgica Tubarão (CST), a full 6,000 miles away.

I was present in Brazil when the first shipment of steel slab was loaded onboard the *Docetaurus* in September 1984. I participated in the design of the supply chain, incorporating innovative approaches to ensure a smooth flow. The ultimate test of a supply chain is its sustainability: CSI's supply chain has been running steadily since 1984.

Managing the Supply Chain

There are many moving parts to a supply chain, and the challenge is how to efficiently manage the points of transfer and points of constriction, also called 'bottlenecks'. My mantra for supply chain management is the '3 V's': *visibility*, *velocity* and *value*. I came up with these during my five years working as supply chain director at the former Redcar Steelworks in northeastern England.

The Redcar blast furnace was the second largest in Europe and required a steady flow of raw materials to be unloaded at the internally-operated deep-water bulk handling port. Five million tons of iron ore and 2.5 million tons of metallurgical coal flowed through the port, coming primarily from Australia, Brazil and the USA. The blast furnace smelted day and night, yielding up to 9,000 tons of liquid iron every 24 hours. The mix to charge the blast furnace consisted of a blend of ores. Given the long supply lines and risk of disruption, inventory on-site was maintained at 90 days of supply. The different varieties of ores and coal had to be kept in extensive stocking yards, and the material needed to be able to be reclaimed to ensure a steady flow.

We developed tracking software that enabled us to predict ship arrivals, allowing for weather and sea conditions. This was important when all the raw materials were arriving at a port with only one berth. If multiple ships arrive simultaneously, the financial consequences can be severe during bull shipping markets: there were times when the daily demurrage cost for keeping a ship waiting was $200,000. Those economics sharpen one's focus on port productivity.

The supply chain can take a severe financial hit from a bottleneck under the wrong conditions. Therefore, the *value* element of the supply chain critically depends on planning to mitigate constriction or bottlenecks. You need to plan on the *velocity* of flow along the supply chain and the factors affecting it. Therefore, supply chain management depends on good metrics to create *visibility*.

There are also internal supply chains to consider, coordinating the flow of cargo into and out of ports with the arrival times of ships. Ports and terminals can hold shipments before loading and after discharge, but they do not have infinite capacity; they have what most terminal operators call their 'optimum capacity', where the available space and equipment perform at their best. When terminals stretch beyond their optimum capacity, they lose efficiency and throughput. For that reason, ports and terminals closely monitor their capacity.

At the Redcar steelworks, the liquid iron was transformed into steel slabs destined for export. Each week, 60,000 tons of freshly-made slabs slid out of the casters. Orders were shipped out to Belgium, Italy, Korea and the USA, each with their own specific sizes and grades. The optimum capacity at the steelworks was one week's production. If the stock levels went higher, it created problems.

The public port was a short distance away, connected by an internal rail link. The trains had to maintain a steady flow of slabs moving down to the port every 24 hours. At the port, the optimum capacity was 75,000 tons. This was sufficient capacity for one full deep-sea cargo of 45,000 tons, plus one 'handy-size' cargo of 20,000 tons and one short sea cargo. The port could simultaneously load one deep-sea and one short-sea ship.

Loading steel slabs in a deep-sea ship (top) and short-sea ship (bottom) in Teesport. David Reid.

On the short-sea ships, a cargo of 6,000 tons loaded in just six hours, and there were times when the last slabs arrived at the port still warm to the touch. They were really fresh! The challenge for the supply chain was to make sure that the last day of production was within four days of the first day of ship loading. Again, *visibility*, *velocity* and *value* formed the guiding principles.

We created a system that increased productivity by more than 100%, reduced the handling costs by 1/3rd and kept average inventory levels at one week of production. This, in turn, ensured a very low 'time-to-cash' metric, the time lag between finishing production and receiving payment from the customer.

The fundamental challenge for everyone involved in managing supply chains is to understand how a delay or a change in flow will impact up and down the line. The recent events of the *Ever Given* blocking the Suez Canal brought this to the public's attention. When a critical artery becomes blocked, even for a short period, the global conveyor grinds to a halt. As ships have become larger to achieve lower transport costs, we also risk having all our eggs in one basket. In prior years, like when I worked on a pre-container general cargo ship, the scale of each shipment was small by comparison to today. We were but a small cog in a large wheel, and if part of the cargo was damaged or lost, there was enough resilience or over-capacity within the system to absorb the loss.

In 1976, as chief mate on the *St Lawrence Prospector*, I was in the Port of Toledo loading a cargo of wheat destined to Norway. The owner of the grain elevator came on board to visit, and we had a conversation about the wheat. He told me that 2% of the cargo was not actually wheat, but grit and other debris. Given that we were loading 18,000 tons, that meant that 360 tons were non-edible. He explained that they had the technology to clean the wheat, but the governing regulations only required 98% purity, so there was no commercial reason to spend the time and effort to ship a perfect product. The 2014 USDA regulations contain similar allowances.

Today, we are mindful of climate change and efficiency. Steps are underway to decarbonize the propulsion systems of the global conveyor. Perhaps new ways will be found to carry only what is essential and minimize waste along the supply chain.

NOTES

1. UNCTAD, 2018. *Review of Maritime Transport 2018.* https://unctad.org/system/files/official-document/ rmt2018ch1_en.pdf. Accessed 2021.

13

PORTS AND PORT AUTHORITIES

Places of Refuge

Seaport by Claude Lorrain, 1638. Public Domain.

In 2013, Ship Technology Global reported that seven of the

world's ten biggest ports by volume were located in China.[1] The ports of Shanghai and Singapore were the largest. The smallest of the ten, the Port of Busan in South Korea, handled about 1/3rd more cargo than the Port of South Louisiana, the largest American port at the time. In fact, the only top-ten port outside of Pacific Asia was the Port of Rotterdam in the Netherlands. This statistic reveals the centrality of Asia to the global supply chain.

The oldest artificial harbor discovered was in Wadi al-Jarf in Egypt, about 74 miles south of Suez on the Red Sea. Archeologists discovered the port in 1832. Excavations revealed a 490 ft jetty built from stone about 4,500 years old and storage galleries carved into the rock face. The port was most likely created to serve the commercial needs of the Pharaohs, supporting the trade of goods in the Red Sea and perhaps even further to the Arabian Gulf and the Indian Ocean.

For much of ancient Rome's history, the harbor of Ostia Antica ('frontmost mouth') at the mouth of the River Tiber was the center of its marine activity. It was also vulnerable to strong winds and storms from the southwest, however, so around 50 AD the Emperor Claudius had a second harbor created. This harbor was called Portus, the Latin word for 'harbor'. This is the root of the English word 'port', now widely used for the shipping real estate that serves as a home for multiple docks, piers and jetties. Portus served the commercial needs of Rome for more than 500 years, and today the site of Portus is near the Roman international airport Fiumicino.

Ports represent the real estate assets of the global shipping industry. They have evolved from simple wharves, capable of berthing only a single ship, into vast swaths of land that often also incorporate the sorting, processing and distribution of products into the retail network.

According to the US Coast Guard, 360 commercial ports serve the needs of shipping in the United States. Canada has 17 port authorities and 31 ports designated as public by the federal government, and Transport Canada also owns and operates many small ports for remote serving communities.

Port Management

Who owns the ports? In some cases, the entire port is owned by one entity, and this can be either in public or private control. In other cases, the port is sub-divided into sections or zones with portions under public ownership operating alongside areas of privately-owned assets.

A few examples illustrate the diversity of port infrastructure. The Port of Antwerp in Belgium is the second largest port in Europe, built under the orders of Napoleon Bonaparte in 1811. It is a classic instance of the 'landlord' model of ports, owned 100% by the City of Antwerp. The landlord port model places the management of the port real estate and the primary port infrastructure with an omnipotent port authority. That port authority then leases areas of the port to private companies, who operate their sections of the port as a private commercial enterprise. This is also the model used by the US ports of

Long Beach and Los Angeles. Like Antwerp, the two
California ports are also owned by their respective city
governments.

Landlord-model port authorities derive revenue from two
basic fees: wharfage, a tariff based on the weight of the
cargo; and dockage, a charge based on the size of the ship
and the duration of its stay within the port. Typically, the
port tenant or lessee will collect the port fees on behalf
of the port authority and pass on either the total amount
or a share to them. In some lease arrangements, the port
authority will lease the port space for a fixed yearly rental,
leaving the private operator free to retain all the fees earned
from wharfage and dockage.

India's main ports were established as port trusts under
the Major Port Trusts Act. They operate under the 'service'
port model, where the port trust performs all port functions.
Some other ports are 'hybrid' operations: the port
authorities have their own operating arms that fulfill all the
tasks otherwise done by a private company, but they can
also lease out port terminals under various arrangements
for private companies to operate. Sometimes they even
compete with their own tenants. One example of this type
of operation is the Teesport in Middlesbrough. The port is
owned by the private company PD Ports, which is itself part
of the larger Canadian asset management firm Brookfield.
PD Ports acts both as a statutory port authority, managing
the entire port complex and leasing parts of it, and as an
operating company, providing direct services to port users.
The Port of Philadelphia is another example of this model.

Waterfront real estate management has evolved into an industry sector of its own. Conferences and seminars on issues like port security and sustainability are held yearly on the global and local levels. In the second half of 2019, there were almost 40 significant conferences focused on ports worldwide. As the CEO of a private port in Pennsylvania, I myself routinely attended at least two port conferences each year. I realized that it would be possible for some port development professionals to spend the entire year just hopping from one conference to the next.

Many of these conferences become hubs for trade fair networking, allowing equipment suppliers and service companies to set up lavish trade booths to display their technology. Ports have large capital budgets to spend on new cranes and civil engineering. In the 1996 movie *Jerry Maguire*, Cuba Gooding Jr famously said, "Show me the money": ports have money flowing into their coffers and are all eager for growth and expansion. Almost every marketing brochure produced by any port authority will describe why their port has strategic advantages to shippers and shipping companies. They vie for each other's business to enable their revenues to grow, and that growth then fuels their future capital expansion.

While world trade does continue to grow as the world population expands, not all ports can sustain steady growth. Some ports that depended on one industry have ballooned in periods of intense activity only for the industry to close its doors. In these cases, the revenue dwindles along with the marketing campaign. The port authority is forced either to reinvent itself or to adopt a survival strategy for minimal business.

Ports for Seafarers

The term 'safe port' has come to have a very specific legal meaning over the years, refined in maritime law by case after case. The classic statement comes from the Lord Justice Frederic Aked Sellers of the UK, in a judgment he gave on the case of the *Eastern City* in 1958:

> A port will not be safe unless, in the relevant period of time, a particular ship can reach it, use it and return from it without, in the absence of some abnormal occurrence, being exposed to danger which cannot be avoided by good navigation and seamanship.[2]

Subsequent court rulings have affirmed the definition.

The terms 'safe port' and 'safe berth' are particularly relevant when ships are chartered and sent to ports and berths that are not part of their regular trading pattern. In the popular New York Produce Exchange (NYPE) contract form, the preamble contains an absolute warranty that the ship "will only be employed between 'safe ports and safe places.'"

'Port of refuge' is another important term. A port of refuge is a port chosen by the master when the ship has to deviate from a voyage because of a threat to the common safety, like shifting cargo, a fire on board, or a severe mechanical failure. A deviation of this nature may trigger a 'general average', an insurance mechanism that requires all parties involved in the voyage to bear a percentage of the expenses incurred by the deviation and repairs. The parties will include the shipowner and the cargo owners, and the fuel on board will have a marine insurance policy that includes coverage for the general average.

In 2008, the MSC *Sabrina* ran aground in the St Lawrence River. The ship was aground in the river for one month while plans were being made to lighten the ship by transferring containers to a sister vessel. The owner of the MSC *Sabrina* claimed general average. As a result, the insurers for the cargo on board shared the cost of the rescue with the owner proportionately to the respective values of the cargo and the ship.

For seafarers, the Maritime Labour Convention (MLC) 2006 established important standards and guidelines concerning welfare facilities at ports:

> Standard A4.4 – Access to shore-based welfare facilities
>
> 1. Each Member shall require, where welfare facilities exist on its territory, that they are available for the use of all seafarers, irrespective of nationality, race, color, sex, religion, political opinion or social origin and irrespective of the flag State of the ship on which they are employed or engaged or work.

2. Each Member shall promote the development of welfare facilities in appropriate ports of the country and determine, after consultation with the shipowners' and seafarers' organizations concerned, which ports are to be regarded as appropriate.

3. Each Member shall encourage the establishment of welfare boards which shall regularly review welfare facilities and services to ensure that they are appropriate in the light of changes in the needs of seafarers resulting from technical, operational and other developments in the shipping industry.[3]

The MLC 2006 also includes guidelines for establishing port welfare boards:

Guideline B4.4.3 – Welfare boards

1. Welfare boards should be established, at the port, regional and national levels, as appropriate. Their functions should include:

(a) keeping under review the adequacy of existing welfare facilities and monitoring the need for the provision of additional facilities or the withdrawal of underutilized facilities; and

(b) assisting and advising those responsible for providing welfare facilities and ensuring coordination between them.

2. Welfare boards should include among their members representatives of shipowners' and seafarers' organizations, the competent authorities and, where appropriate, voluntary organizations and social bodies.

3. As appropriate, consuls of maritime States and local representatives of foreign welfare organizations should, in accordance with national laws and regulations, be associated with the work of port, regional and national welfare boards.[4]

Ports should be a place of safety and refuge for the ship and the seafarer, each for their individual needs. The owners and operators of ports have their commercial priorities and are often competing against each other. For the master, the port and the assigned berth need to be safe and fit for the intended purpose. For every seafarer, there is the aspiration of shore leave and the opportunity to seek assistance from the seafarer missions and other voluntary welfare organizations. Port managers and administrations have to be mindful of the needs of seafarers; all their business and revenue depends on them.

NOTES

1. Ship Technology Global, 2013. "The world's 10 biggest ports". https://www.ship-technology.com/features/feature-the-worlds-10-biggest-ports/. Accessed 2021.

2. 1958. *Leeds Shipping Company, Ltd v Société Française Bunge*. 2 Lloyd's Rep. 127.

3. International Labour Organization, 2006. *Maritime Labour Convention*.

4. ibid.

14

STEVEDORES AND CONTAINERS

―――∾∾―――

Loading Up

Longshoremen on a New York dock loading
barrels of corn syrup onto a barge on the Hudson.
Lewis Hine, c. 1912. Public Domain.

Rose George, author of *Ninety Percent of Everything*,
describes the business of shipping as "the system that
delivers clothes on your back, gas in your car, and food on
your plate".[1] Seafarers manage and guide the ships from port
to port, but, for the most part, when ships are in port the
task of loading and unloading cargo rests with a shore-based
workforce. There are some exceptions where specialized
ships are capable of self-unloading, but even in these cases
the ship has to liaise with a shore terminal. Tankers are the
predominant type of self-unloading ship, using shipboard
pumps to send their cargo into pipelines that flow into the
shoreside tanks. Even though the ship is controlling the
flow, however, the refinery or tank farm will dictate the rate
at which they can receive. When the cargo is being loaded

on, even tankers and self-unloading bulk carriers rely on the shore terminal; there is no such thing as a self-loading ship.

The word 'stevedore' originated in Portugal as *estivador*, 'loader'. In the United Kingdom the word was 'docker'; in the United States and Canada, the word was 'longshoreman'. Since the days of wooden ships driven by sail, the cargo carried by ships has required these workers' skills of stowage and the art of stevedoring to fit cargo safely and efficiently inside the compartments of a ship. This work began as the physically challenging manual tasks of carrying cargo onboard or passing it across the ship's rail. This process was improved by the use of rigging a derrick with lifting tackle, which allowed for heavier lifts and faster work. The early iterations still required manual winching of the tackle to raise and lower the hook, however.

A Canadian self-unloader with a 250 ft boom. David Reid.

Since those days, the demands of world trade have continuously required more shipping capacity. This gave rise in the early 19th century to steel-hulled cargo ships, still powered by sail, and in the early 20th century to the fast clipper ships that plied the ocean routes.

The barque *Moshulu* c. 2005. N. Johannes. Public Domain.

The four-masted steel barque *Moshulu*, now in service as a restaurant at Penn's Landing in Philadelphia, represents a perfect example of the cargo ship of 100 years past. The *Moshulu* could carry just 5,300 tons of cargo, compared to the 150,000-ton capacity of the container ships that frequent our modern container terminals.

The relationship between seafarers and the small army of people that load and unload the ship has always been a symbiotic arrangement: the business of stowage, while performed by the stevedores, is at the direction of the ship's deck officers.

Stevedore managers are often former seafarers who left the sea for a shoreside job. Seafarers interact with the stevedores as they come onboard and when hatches need to be opened or cargo lights are needed for night work. The relationship between seafarers and stevedores is universal because it works the same in every port in every nation.

Intermodal Revolution

The system of handling cargo has changed dramatically with the introduction of mechanized handling systems, reducing the need for physical labor. Some 65 years ago, prior to the ISO container, all cargo was shipped either loose in boxes or crates or made up into unit loads on pallets. The task of loading and unloading the individual boxes and crates and pallets was the work of stevedores. Today, the movement of general cargo is the domain of the shipping container and its unit of measure, the 20 ft-equivalent unit (teu). The original teu was a steel container measuring 8 ft high, 8 ft wide and 20 ft long.

The history of the shipping container leads back to the railroads, who recognized that it was more efficient to move cargo inside a unitized container. In the early 1950s, the US Army began unitizing loads with the CONEX box system, enabling military supplies to be moved efficiently. The real patriarch of today's container revolution, however, is Malcom McLean.

McLean's first containers were only 10 ft in length. A trucker from North Carolina, his initial interest in shipping was to create ships capable of transporting his truck semi-trailers up and down the US Atlantic Coast corridor. Soon, however, McLean realized that it would be far more efficient if he could separate the box from the chassis of the trailer. In 1955, he worked together with design engineer Keith Tantlinger to create a rectangular shipping container with twist lock fittings at each corner. These twist locks made a simple connection between box and chassis and also provided a simple system for lifting and securing. They still remain the keystone of every facet of the global container handling system in the 21st century.

To further his dream, in 1956 McLean acquired two World War II T-2 tankers and converted them to carry his intermodal containers on deck. The first voyage took place in April 1956, with the SS *Ideal-X* sailing from Port Newark to Houston carrying 58 of McLean's intermodal containers. In April 1960, McLean's Pan-Atlantic Steamship Corporation became SeaLand; it would go on to become one of the great leviathans of the global container industry.

McLean's gift to the world was making his patents for standardized container design available at no cost to the International Organization for Standardization (ISO). In so doing, he enabled a super-efficient system of intermodal transport embraced world- and industry-wide. Railroads with double-stack container trains weave across the Western US and connect China and Europe under the Chinese Belt and Road network. The system of unitized containers that began with the railroads has now come full circle.

McLean's intermodal revolution changed life on the docks around the world forever. In the 1970's, redundancy threatened all port workers as the use of his ISO containers expanded rapidly. In the 21st century, the work remains; however, the size of the workforce is greatly diminished, and the physical labor has been largely replaced by mechanized handling methods. The cost of handling cargo has reduced dramatically with the reduced need for labor, and efficiency has increased, reducing time in port and time to market. Further savings came from reductions in damage and loss, since the cargo is now sealed inside the ISO container from shipper to receiver. By some estimates, employment in the ports dropped by 90% following the intermodal revolution.

Stevedores at Work

In 1969, I joined the *London Statesman*, a British general cargo ship, in Brooklyn, New York. The *Statesman* was under charter to the American shipping company States Marine Lines and employed in their US-to-Far East liner service. Each round trip from New York lasted five and a half months and no ISO containers were carried: every piece of cargo was loaded and discharged by multiple gangs of longshoremen. The design of the docks in Brooklyn was similar to many US ports, with the dock warehouse sited close to the edge of the wharf with two levels for receiving cargo. The outboard ship's derrick was swung out to enable the cargo net to land at either the lower or upper level of the warehouse. Cargo in the net was then manhandled on to hand trucks and moved into the warehouse. In later years, a wooden pallet would be used so that a small forklift could replace the use of hand trucks.

Onboard the ship, we could work up to nine gangs of

longshoremen. Each gang consisted of 18 men total: ten men in the hold, two winchmen, a hatch tender and a foreman onboard, and four men on the dock. Every morning at 8 am, as many as 120 burly longshoremen made their way up the *Statesman*'s gangway to take up position in our holds and on deck. At midday they left for lunch and returned at 1 pm for the afternoon shift. This small army took over the ship every day.

In the summer of 1969, we spent three weeks alongside in Brooklyn. There was no night or weekend work due to the high cost of overtime for the longshoremen. The bulk of our 15,000 tons of cargo was consumer products: the descriptions of contents on the cardboard boxes told us we carried transistor radios, 8-track players, Christmas decorations, plastic flowers, clothing and all manner of other goods. This was the supply line that fed Sears, Roebuck and Woolworths, the main street stores of the time.

Labor supply in ports is predominantly represented by trade unions, with the pay, terms and conditions negotiated under master agreements with the shipping lines and stevedoring companies. These companies are confusingly themselves also sometimes called 'stevedores'.

Employment in the ports has always fluctuated. The demand for labor can ebb and flow as the number of ships in port rises and falls. For this reason, the labor supply is managed from a labor pool or hiring hall. Longshoremen and dockers are paid only on the days when they work; they are not on a salary system, although some labor agreements contained guaranteed annual income protection. To cope with surges in labor demand, the union members are the first to receive work from the labor pool; once they are fully employed, the workforce can be supplemented by the use of 'casuals' who are outside the union membership. The method of hiring varies, but as a general rule those with the lower hours to date are called first, so that there is a fairness of earning capability.

Some ports used the 'parent gang' system, where each stevedoring company sponsored a number of gangs known by the names of their foremen. The company had first call on their sponsored gangs, ensuring that they had continuity of skill for their particular operation. If that company needed more gangs, they could pull from the other available gangs not called out.

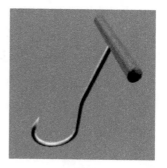

Longshoreman's hook, self-made. 8 May 2008, Anthony Appleyard. Public Domain.

Other ports use an hours-worked dispatch system, and gangs are made up from the hiring hall on an ad-hoc basis. When I worked in the Port of Long Beach, California, at the start of a ship unloading the first shift was always a challenge, because the individuals making up each gang had to assemble and get to know each other as they formed into a gang to work the ship: something that the parent gang system did not require. In my own experience having worked with both systems, the parent gang system was safer, because the members of the gang always worked together just like seafarers do onboard a ship.

In our ports today, we have a much smaller workforce than the pre-McLean days of the 1950s. The radical change has been the capital investment and quantum of mechanical handling equipment that now operates in the ports, from the post-Panamax gantry and mobile harbor cranes to the reach stackers and high capacity fork-lift trucks. In the port of the 21st century, the stevedores, dockers and longshoremen have traded in their cargo hook for a seat in a multi-million-dollar machine.

NOTES

1. 2013. *Ninety Percent of Everything.* New York: Henry and Holt Co.

15

CANALS AND LOCKS

---∽---

Shipping Shortcuts

Courses of the Grand Canal of
China. CC BY-SA 4.0.

Canals are the shortcuts ships use to travel overland. Locks in canals provide ships with a constant water-depth over different elevations. Significant tidal variations often make it necessary for ships to enter the locks from a tidal river, but within the lock, the water level remains constant within the enclosed harbor. There are many locks in use in Europe, including in the ports of Antwerp, Amsterdam and Ghent. It takes time to transit through locks, however, and port expenses are higher, so ports with lock access have a handicap compared to ports with direct sea access.

Canals for transport date back as far as the 5th century BC with the Jing-Hang Grand Canal in China. The Grand Canal extends for 1,776 km and remains in active use.

The modern, two-gated 'pound' lock system was invented in China in the 10th century AD. A chamber with gates at each end enables barges and ships to move from one canal elevation to another. The first European pound lock was built in the late 14th century, near Bruges in Belgium. In the 15th century, Leonardo da Vinci designed the first 'miter' gates, which meet and form chevrons pointing upstream and then are held shut by the upstream water pressure.

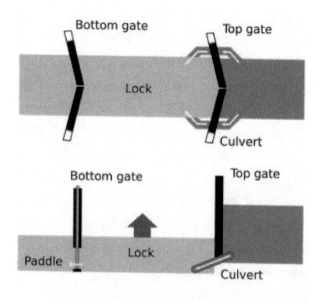

Locks with miter and pound gates. CC BY-SA 3.0.

The largest lock in the world is the Kieldrecht Lock, opened in 2016, which connects the Scheldt River with the left bank harbor of Antwerp. The Kieldrecht is 500 m long and 68 m wide, with an operational depth of 17.8 m. The locks created in the Panama Canal under the Panama Canal Expansion project, which were also opened in 2016, are 427 m long and 55 m wide with a depth of 18.3 m. In addition, a new and even larger lock is under construction and will open in 2022 at Ijmuiden to serve the Port of Amsterdam.

Mediterranean/Indian: The Suez Canal

The Suez Canal is a sea-level waterway connecting Port Said on Egypt's Mediterranean coast with the Gulf of Suez on its Indian coast. Before the Suez Canal, ships traveling between Europe and Asia had to circumnavigate south of Africa, passing the Cape of Good Hope in South Africa to reach the Indian Ocean. For a ship sailing from Singapore to Antwerp, the Suez Canal represents a shortcut of 6,000 km.

The Suez Canal opened for business on November 17, 1869. The 193 km waterway was constructed between 1859 and 1869 by the Suez Canal Company, created by the French diplomat Ferdinand de Lesseps. The Egyptian government owned the canal, but its operation was conceded to British and French shareholders until the Egyptian Government nationalized it in 1956. This move triggered the Suez Crisis, a joint invasion by Britain, France and Israel in November 1956 in which thousands died before it was ended by international pressure.

Opening of the Suez Canal, 1869. Public Domain.

By treaty, the Suez Canal is open to all nations in times of war and peace, but the Egyptian Government still closed the canal on June 5, 1967, when the Six-Day War with Israel began, and did not reopen it again until June 5, 1975.

Today, the Suez Canal has been expanded to increase capacity, and ships are piloted in groups or convoys daily, one from each end. The convoys pass in the two parallel channels north of Great Bitter Lake. The transit from Port Said to Suez takes approximately 12 hours. It is estimated to handle approximately 12% of global trade, and the tolls collected from shipowners contribute 10% of the Egyptian GDP. In addition, the revenue from the Suez Canal is the number-three foreign currency revenue category for Egypt.

Pacific/Atlantic: Panama Canal

The Panama Canal provides a connection between the Atlantic and Pacific Oceans. Before it opened in 1914, ships travelling from one side to the other had to make the much longer voyage around Cape Horn at the southern tip of South America; with the Canal, it is a mere eight hours from lock to lock.

Construction of locks on the Panama Canal, 1913.
Public Domain.

The first attempt to construct the Panama Canal was led by Ferdinand de Lesseps, the same man who successfully built the Suez Canal. Although work began in 1881, it was challenging, and thousands of workers died due to tropical diseases. By the time Lesseps' project fell into bankruptcy in 1889, 20,000 workers had perished. In 1894 a second French company called the New Panama Canal Company took over the project with a new plan. In 1904, it, too, gave up on its project and decided to sell its equipment to the Americans. Over the next ten years, the United States Government succeeded in building the first Panama Canal and opened it in 1914. In 1999, the Panama Canal Authority assumed control of the canal from the United States. Panama derives 10% of its GDP from the revenues earned by ships passing through the canal.

Location of the Panama Canal between the Pacific and Caribbean. Public Domain.

The bottleneck for the 1914 Panama Canal eventually grew to be the size of its locks, and ships began to outgrow the canal's maximum ('Panamax') beam of 106 ft. The Panamanian Government approved an expansion project, and construction began in 2007. New locks allowing for wider, longer and deeper ships to transit between both major oceans opened on June 26, 2016.

145

Great Lakes/Atlantic: St Lawrence Seaway and Soo Locks

The St Lawrence Seaway and Soo Locks create a path for ships from the Atlantic to navigate the five Great Lakes, making it possible for ships to reach deep into the US Midwest and the Canadian province of Ontario. The present seaway was officially opened on June 26, 1959. The joint US and Canadian scheme replaced a smaller Canadian canal and lock system that dated back to the 19th century.

The Wiley-Dondero Canal and Snell lock (USA) on the St Lawrence Seaway. Public Domain.

The journey starts at the Montréal to Lake Ontario section, which comprises a series of canals 306 km long, raising ships by 75 m over the course of seven single locks. The route meanders along the US-Canadian border, with five of the locks in Canada and two in the United States. After leaving the St Lawrence River at Montréal, ships reach the east end of Lake Ontario. From there, they can sail on to the entrance to the Welland Canal at the west end of Lake Ontario, where they pass through eight locks to reach Lake Erie, rising a further 99 m over a distance of 43 km. All of the Welland Canal locks are in Canada. Most are single locks, but the Locks 4, 5 and 6 are a series of 'double flight' locks in which ships can pass each other. From Lake Erie, ships can go via the Detroit River, past the cities of Detroit and Windsor and the southern end of Lake Huron. At the northern end of Lake Huron, ships can either go west through the Mackinac straits to Lake Michigan or transit the American-controlled Soo Locks in St Marys River to reach Lake Superior.

The St Lawrence Seaway has ship size restrictions known as Seaway-max, limiting the length to 225.5 m, a maximum beam of 23.77 m and a draft of 8.08 m in freshwater. The Soo Locks are larger and allow ships up to 304 m long to trade between Lakes Superior, Michigan, Huron and Erie. US-flag ore carriers, which can navigate the Soo Locks, but are too large to use the Welland Canal. They are therefore captive to the Upper Lakes: their principal trade is moving iron ore from Minnesota to the steel plants in Chicago, Detroit and Cleveland. This was the exact route followed by the *Edmund Fitzgerald*, which sank during a November 1975 storm in Lake Superior.

The St Lawrence Seaway closes to navigation for essential maintenance from late December to late March. The captive Great Lakes fleet of ships goes into layup during these winter months.

Gulf of St Lawrence/Atlantic: Canso Canal

The Canso Canal and Lock in Nova Scotia, Canada enables ships to avoid traveling around Cape Breton Island

and passing the Cabot Strait. It was constructed between 1953 and 1955. A single Seaway-max lock allows any vessel capable of transiting the St Lawrence Seaway to fit through the Canso Canal.

Canso Canal Lock. Dennis Jarvis. CC BY-SA 2.0.

Baltic/North Sea: Kiel Canal

The Kiel Canal, formerly known as the Kaiser Wilhelm Canal, extends 98 km across Germany's northern state of Schleswig-Holstein, helping ships avoid having to navigate around Denmark. It is accessed via a set of locks at Brunsbüttel, at the mouth of the Elbe River on the North Sea, and another set of locks at Kiel-Holtenau, on the Baltic. The canal opened in 1895 and was widened in 1914 to accommodate German naval battleships. It can currently handle Panamax-size vessels, but is limited to a maximum draft of 9.5 m.

Adventures on Waterways

During my time at sea, I passed through the Panama

Canal many times, with my first time being on Christmas Day 1968. I have made many transits of the St Lawrence Seaway, on both British and Canadian flag ships and have also passed through the Kiel and the Canso canals. I never experienced the Suez Canal, though, as its eight-year closure corresponded almost exactly to my years at sea.

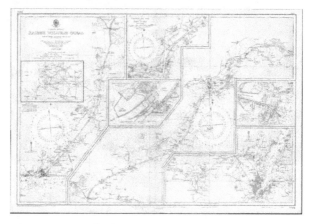

The Kaiser Wilhelm Canal on an Admiralty Chart c. 1920. Public Domain.

I had one memorable weekend on the Welland Canal in the summer of 1975. I was chief mate on the *Ontario Power*, and we were upbound in Lock 7 of the Welland Canal loaded with a cargo of coal. I was in radio contact with the bridge from my station on the bow. We entered the lock, and I was chatting with the lockmaster on the lock wall above me.

When a ship enters a lock, it has to push its way forward. As the water tries to find a way out, the ship's hull displaces the water in the lock chamber. As chief mate, I was advising the master piloting on the bridge on how much further we needed to advance. I was receiving my guidance from the lockmaster. We were down to the last 20 ft, and I was looking directly at the lock wall. It was easy for me to observe the lock wall and monitor our progress. "Twenty feet to go", I advised the master.

To my surprise, instead of moving ahead, we suddenly started to move astern. The lockmaster, expecting that we were almost in position, had already begun to close the lock gates astern of us, and the safety cable had already been lowered.

The lockmaster was now very agitated, and I radioed the bridge again. Moments later, there was a crashing and wrenching sound. The *Ontario Power* came to a complete stop and was now fouled and intertwined with the lock's safety cable, into which it had collided. The large-diameter wire cable was designed to protect the lock gates from damage and did its job: we missed the gates by inches. Lock 7 is a single lock, so we brought the entire Welland Canal to a standstill that Sunday. The *Ontario Power* was damaged, including our port lifeboat, which had to be removed for repairs. It took until the next day to complete all the surveys and inspections, remove the cable and fit extra rafts to compensate for our damaged lifeboat.

Fortunately nobody was injured. Our 3rd cook, who had been peeling potatoes at the rear galley door, had been the closest person to the stern. He dropped his peeling knife and ran in the right direction when he heard the impact.

The cause of the problem was traced to a fault in the bridge control system that allowed the master to control the steam turbine engine directly. The master had rung for 'slow ahead', but in the engine room, it did the opposite, 'slow astern'. That was why we started going the wrong way. When the master realized the problem, he gave a double ring, but they misunderstood him as wanting emergency full astern, so they went to manual control and increased it to maximum. By the time the master called the engine room and the engine was stopped it was too late.

Canals and locks provide great fascination for tourists. They make it possible to reach inland ports and create economic benefits for the shipowner and the countries that host them. However, they always involve a lot of extra work for seafarers.

16

DRY DOCKING

This summer, I enjoyed riding my bike along the bank of
the River Adour in Bayonne, France. The path is part of
the EuroVelo 1 bike route, which extends along Europe's
Atlantic coasts from Spain to Ireland to Norway. I like how
these dedicated bike paths, or _voies-vertes_, allow you to weave
your way through urban and industrial areas; it is rather like
traveling on a canal boat.

The Port of Bayonne and the naval base are situated on
the south side of the river, and there is a small dry dock that
is easily viewed from the bike path. On my first ride, there
was a small dredger resting on the dry dock's blocks; a few
days later, the dredger was gone, and the dock was dry. I
took the opportunity to explain to my wife the mechanics of
dry docking a ship.

Dry docks are structures in which ships can be built, inspected and maintained out of the water. Before the ship enters a dry dock, giant concrete or timber blocks are placed along the floor of the dry dock in accordance with the plan of the ship itself, and then the dry dock is filled with water. The ship navigates into the dry dock, the water is drained out, and the ship rests on the blocks while work is performed on it. The most common dry docks encountered by merchant seafarers are gated structures built into the land, called 'graving docks'. There are also 'floating docks' that pump water in and out of their own floors and walls: they weigh themselves down with water to partially submerge and get under a ship and then pump the water out to lift the ship up with them. Floating docks are most commonly used for salvaging ships.

A certain trim is needed in order to enter a dry dock, so the crew needs to ballast the ship to keep it at the right level. The ship is very carefully manipulated into the dock. The gate is closed, and then the dock begins pumping out the water. While this happens, the ship has to be kept in a precise position so that the hull balances properly on the keel blocks down the center of the dock. The stern has to make contact first. The all-important moment comes when the ship transfers from floating to resting statically on the keel blocks.

Once the hull has fully rested on the keel blocks, the rest of the water can be pumped out. Power is connected from the shore because the ship's generators have to be shut down. Multiple shore gangways are placed, because there will be a lot of pedestrian traffic each day as the shipyard workers come and go.

Staying at the Shipyard

My first experience of dry docking was on the *London Prestige* in 1969, at the Mitsui Shipyard in Tamano, Japan. After making the pilotage through the Seto Inland Sea, we arrived in the bay opposite the shipyard. It was late afternoon when we anchored, despite the lateness of the day. From the anchorage, the yard took over and used their tugs to move us to the waiting dock. Teams of shipyard workers streamed up the gangway, with the majority heading into the engine room. At the same time as we were being manipulated into the dock, down in the engine room, there were scores of women wiping down our engine in preparation for overhaul.

We spent two weeks at Tamano, and each day would begin with music playing over the shipyard loudspeakers. This was the cue for the daily warm-up exercises undertaken by every shipyard worker. As soon as the music started, they would stop wherever they were and wait for the exercise mantra to begin. Then, for about ten minutes, everyone in view would be swinging their arms, touching their toes and getting fit. We decided to join in, so shortly after seven each morning before breakfast, we assembled on deck and followed along.

We were able to remain living onboard, but we could not shower. So, in the evening, we gathered our towels and toiletries and walked to the shipyard bathhouse building as a group. This was very elegant and set up in the Japanese bathhouse style. We learned that you soak in the big pool, but you do not use any soap; that is reserved for use in the shower. The whole experience was very relaxing, and those evening visits to the bathhouse were truly memorable. I returned a few years later to Tamano on another ship, and it was again an excellent experience.

I cannot say the same about the experience of a dry docking at the port of Falmouth in Southern England, however. I was onboard a hard-working products tanker that spent most of its time on very short shuttle voyages moving fuel around in northern Europe. We arrived in Falmouth after a stormy trip down the Irish Sea from Liverpool, cleaning our tanks around the clock to have them gas-free before the docking. As it happened, this was not a significant problem, because our prior cargo had been a very waxy crude that had to be heated to keep it pumpable. We had almost 6 ft of oil remaining in one of our center tanks that we had been unable to pump because it was so viscous. The oil went solid as the temperature dropped to the ambient UK winter weather, and we passed gas-free without any problem. I remember being inside the tank and walking around on the surface of the oil. It was like a black moonscape.

The work practices at the Falmouth yard were in direct contrast to Tamano. In the dark winter morning, the shipyard workers would shuffle onboard. There was no exercise program in Falmouth. Once they were on board, they all seemed to disappear until it was time for the lunch break. When we left the yard in Falmouth, there was a consensus among us that our ship was in worse condition than when we arrived.

Dry Docks at Work

During dry docking, one of the principal tasks is to repair all the items that cannot be tackled when the ship is afloat: repacking the stern tube around the main drive shaft to the propeller, for example, or cleaning and checking the sea chests that allow the entry of seawater for cooling in the engine room. Then there is the formidable task of cleaning and repainting the underwater portion of the hull. It takes days to high-pressure wash the vast surface area. The underside and lower hull are done using airless systems that pump the paint under pressure through the application nozzle. The best ambient conditions for painting are rare.

Even the area directly underneath the hull, in between the keel blocks on which the ship is resting, needs to be washed and inspected. The keel blocks allow enough height to walk under the hull and inspect the bottom plating comfortably. It is an eerie experience to walk underneath your ship, knowing that the ship's total weight is resting on the blocks: you are walking around in the middle of the sandwich.

One of the last jobs of dry docking is inspecting the drain plugs beneath each double bottom tank used for ballast. These are removed to drain the tanks fully and then refitted, so it is essential to make sure they all are in place before the dock is flooded.

Time spent in a dry dock is not cheap, and in addition, there is lost revenue from the ship being out of service. Commercial pressures keep the painting going on even though the temperature may be cool and the weather uncooperative. The reality is that once the dock has been flooded, very little of the hull will be visible except for the boot topping and topsides, and they can be touched up by the crew as needed using a roller on a bamboo pole.

My most prolonged period at a shipyard was undergoing a major engine refit over a winter season in Hamburg. While at the yard, we took advantage of the opportunity to have several other minor maintenance jobs resolved without the usual hectic rush in a typical dry docking. After our two M.A.N. medium-speed diesel engines had been rebuilt, we needed to do engine trials. The ship was an ice-class 1 Panamax bulk carrier with two engines driving a single propeller: a lot of horsepower to test. The first attempt was made at mooring dolphins in the Elbe River. We secured ourselves with as many lines as we could and began testing, but the high power quickly overwhelmed the moorings, and this idea had to be abandoned.

The decision was then made to head out and do trials in the North Sea. It was March in Hamburg, and the damp cold of the North Sea wind cuts through your layers of clothing like a knife. As chief mate, I was delighted to stand down from my station on the forecastle. We came back into the Elbe with the plan to berth in Brunsbüttel near the entrance to the Kiel Canal. The river pilot decided to drop the port anchor to assist with the turn off the berth. I let the anchor go at the bridge's command, but we were moving too quickly and it got caught on the riverbed. The windlass brake shuddered, the cable snapped, and we lost the anchor and about five shackles of chain into the river. We had almost completed a ten-month rebuild of the engines, and then this happened. As so often happens in the world of shipping, we asked ourselves what would happen next.

The highly efficient German tugs brought us alongside at Brunsbüttel. While the main engine received its final tune-up, our anchor and cable were retrieved from the bottom of the Elbe and laid out on the dock. We fitted a new connecting link and winched it back on board to safekeeping in the chain locker. After that experience, I realized that the size of our ship and the strength of the anchor cables needed to be given due consideration before trying to use them as brakes. When we finally left the Elbe and headed towards the Dover Straits, we eagerly looked forward to warmer climates and the twists and turns of navigating the Orinoco River in Venezuela.

When a ship is launched, it becomes buoyant for the first time. From that point on, through its entire commercial life, it enjoys a buoyant relationship with water, whether fresh, salt, or brine. When dry docked, a ship is out of its natural state and its onboard systems are interrupted. The transition from buoyancy to taking the blocks is like a hospital patient being placed on life support. When that intubation is over, it takes time to bring everything back to normal. For the mariner, a dry docking is rather like an intensive hospitalization, and, in the days that follow after a dry docking, mariners become its nurses.

17

FLAGS AND
REGISTRIES

Bunting

The Red Ensign. David Reid.

The maritime tradition of flying flags has remained the same for centuries. Bunting, the fabric traditionally used to make flags, goes back to the 18th century, when it consisted of wool dyed to the required color and then stitched together to form the required distinctive pattern. Flags are manually connected to a halyard and hoisted into position. This tradition is one of the jobs that has yet to be automated and seafarers are still needed for.

Every nation has a national flag that can be easily recognized from a distance, and maritime signal flags represent the alphabet letters and numbers. There are also special maritime flags, called ensign flags, to distinguish between a merchant and military ships. In place of the Union Jack, British merchant ships fly the Red Ensign or 'Red Duster' at the stern, while a British naval ship will fly the White Ensign.

Flags display the identity of the nation of registry and also show respect to the country of the port that the ship is visiting. In the wheelhouse of every ship, there is a flag locker containing a complete set of the national flags required for the trading route. On some ships that trade on irregular routes, this will mean a portfolio of many national flags.

In addition to the national flags, every ship carries a complete set of alphabet and number flags. When used alone, each of the alphabet flags has different meanings, designed as a universal code of maritime communication. These are joined together to form a message or used individually to indicate a specific activity. Some of the common uses are the red-and-white 'H' flag, which means 'I have a pilot onboard'; the solid yellow 'Q' flag, 'I request free pratique' (access to the port on condition of not carrying disease); and the red 'B' flag with a white triangle cutting into it, 'I have dangerous cargo' (typically this flag is displayed during bunkering operations).

When a merchant ship passes a navy ship at close quarters, there is a custom that the merchant ship will dip its ensign flag as a mark of respect, and the navy ship will respond. My first experience of this came one day in January 1969 at the Port of Kaohsiung, Taiwan. Kaohsiung was in use as a naval base for the United States Navy

Sailing ships dressed overall with maritime signal flags. CC BY 3.0.

during the Vietnam War. As we made our approach, a US Navy destroyer was heading out. I was a navigating cadet manning the bell book on the bridge. Our master said, "He is getting ready to dip his flag, cadet to the ensign now." I had to run as fast as I could down to the main deck and then aft to the stern. I grabbed the halyard for our Red Ensign and slowly lowered it to the half-mast 'dip' position. Across from me, an American sailor dressed in white lowered the Stars and Stripes. It only lasted for a few seconds as our ships slipped past each other, and then both flags were hoisted back to their full position. Onboard the destroyer, they probably had a sailor designated for this simple task; on our merchant ship, I had to scramble. But I was delighted to have pulled it off at the right time.

The flag flown at the stern of a merchant ship is more than just a piece of colored cloth; it represents the nation where the ship is registered. The port of registry is shown on the stern of every ship. The ship's IMO (International Maritime Organization) number will also be prominently displayed on the stern or the superstructure. IMO numbers were introduced in 1987 to create a universal ship identification system. The system became mandatory in 1996, with every ship assigned a unique number that remains with it for life, irrespective of registry and ownership. All of the ship's certificates carry the IMO number. Before IMO numbers, ships were given official numbers assigned by their flag state. The IMO registry is managed on behalf of IMO by IHS Maritime, based in the United Kingdom.

A ship's registry signifies the nation-state whose laws govern it. For most of maritime history, there were traditional maritime nations with organic fleets of commercial shipping operated by citizens of the nation. These maritime nations would also be the ones that invested in the infrastructure to train mariners and technological advances in ship design and operation. China is now the leading maritime nation in the world. However, since the 1950s, alternate open registry systems have evolved.

Open registries have no requirement for the ship to be crewed by citizens or residents of the nation or flag state. Some shipowners changed the registries of their ships to open registry to take advantage of the flexibility they offer. One such advantage is that the shipowner can minimize or eliminate liability for income tax because the nation of registry offers tax incentives.

In the colonial era, European shipowners began recognizing the economic advantages of employing ratings from countries under their control. The Portuguese pioneered this with the use of ratings from their colony of Goa. They were known at the time as 'lascars', a broad definition covering ratings from the entire Indian subcontinent. At the outset of World War I, there were over 50,000 lascars employed on British merchant ships. The British Merchant Shipping Acts of the late 19th and early 20th century were drafted with special regulations for lascars working on British ships under the Red Ensign. During the years that I served on British ships flying the Red Ensign, all of the ships owned by my employer headquartered in London were operated by ratings from Hong Kong, India, or the Philippines. The tankers always had Indian ratings and the general cargo ships had Filipinos.

As commercial pressure on running costs increased, most British shipowners changed their ships' flags to open-registry. The marketplace for officers on open-registry ships trained by other nations expanded. The collapse of the

Soviet Union in 1991 opened up another source of well-trained officers from the former independent states, many eager to take up positions on open registry ships with wages paid in US dollars.

Lascars at the Royal Albert Dock in London, 1936.
CC BY-SA 4.0.

Life with Open Registries

I experienced life under an open-registry when my Canadian employer appointed me to serve as chief mate on the *Phosphore Conveyor*, a Liberian-flagged bulk carrier. I had a Canadian certificate of competency. When I joined the *Conveyor* in Hamburg, all the Canadian officers visited the Liberian consulate in Hamburg, and we were issued Liberian certificates of competency based on our Canadian certificates. The consulate printed them off and handed us a laminated copy. I spent the next six months under the Liberian flag.

My pay, living and working conditions were unaffected.

The ship was owned by a joint venture of Canadian and US interests, and had been purpose-built in Japan to serve a unique trade carrying ores between ports in Venezuela, the US and Canada. The flexibility of the Liberian flag meant that the owners had complete freedom of the nationals that they employed. We sailed with Canadian and British officers and ratings from Barbados. I personally never experienced any deficiency in safety standards or regulatory compliance throughout this time.

The dark side of open-registry is that there is a risk that nations who offer ship registry as a source of revenue with no supporting maritime infrastructure may lack robust flag state oversight. The loss of the Liberian-flagged *Amoco Cadiz* in 1978 off the coast of Brittany in France brought about significant change regarding ship inspections to create enhanced regulatory oversight. In 1982, 14 European nations created the Paris Memorandum on Port State Control (MOU). The Paris MOU set in motion a system of independent inspections of ships irrespective of their flag state. By visiting any port within the scope of the Paris MOU, the ship became subject to inspection. Deficiencies found had to be rectified, and in extreme cases, ships would be detained until the owners completed the work.

While working as the supply chain director at the Redcar steelworks, I saw firsthand the impact of the Paris MOU. A North Korean flagged ship, the *Hyok Sin 2*, was chartered to load a full cargo of steel. While the 25,000 tons of steel were being loaded, the ship was under port state control, so the UK Coastguard conducted an inspection and discovered a series of serious defects. Loading was completed on the second day in the port, but the UK Coastguard detained the ship. The following day the UK Coastguard advised that the ship had a record of defects within the Paris MOU. As a result, the ship could no longer load a cargo and depart from a European port. Instructions were given to discharge the entire cargo, and the Italian charterers and consignees of the steel arrested the ship as security for the cost of the labor (c. $450k).

The *Hyok Sin 2* was put under admiralty arrest pending payment of claims. It remained alongside for two months while its many defects were corrected, and after the North Korean shipowners paid the claims against them, the arrest was lifted. The *Hyok Sin 2* was banned from any other European port and sailed away in ballast. Actions like these enforcing port state control under the Paris MOU may seem extreme, but they send a clear message that non-compliance is not acceptable.

The Paris MOU publishes information about their work, and there are now 27 member nations[1]: Belgium, Bulgaria, Canada, Croatia, Cyprus, Denmark, Estonia, Finland, France, Germany, Greece, Iceland, Ireland, Italy, Latvia, Lithuania, Malta, the Netherlands, Norway, Poland, Portugal, Romania, the Russian Federation, Slovenia, Spain, Sweden and the UK. The Paris MOU website, parismou.org, states the following about itself:

Mission is to eliminate the operation of substandard ships through a harmonized system of port State control.

Annually more than 17.000 inspections take place on board foreign ships in the Paris MoU ports, ensuring that these ships meet international safety, security and environmental standards, and that crew members have adequate living and working conditions.

Basic principle is that the prime responsibility for compliance with the requirements laid down in the international maritime conventions lies with the shipowner/operator. Responsibility for ensuring such compliance remains with the flag State.[2]

The website of the Paris MOU provides transparency and open access for anyone to view the current list of ships detained, giving the name of the ship, the IMO number, flag state, date and port of detention. There is also a list of ships banned from access to the ports covered by the Paris MOU.

The rules are clearly defined, and ships will be banned. The detention of the *Hyok Sin 2* at Teesside was its third detention event, moving the ship to the banned list. The master and owners were aware that they were at risk due to the two prior detentions. Despite this, the owners failed to take corrective action. Perhaps they hoped to avoid inspection. The combined costs incurred by the shipowners to pay the claim for loading, repairs, and the loss of revenue from the detention and sailing away in ballast demonstrates that the lower cost option is always to ensure compliance.

There is always the possibility that a port state control inspection will pick up something that needs to be corrected on any ship. This must be viewed with a positive attitude. A second set of eyes checking on safety and regulations creates a partnership that is in the common interest. A good port state control inspector will demonstrate a qualified, professional approach in support of good seamanship. Seafarers are subject to many inspection regimes, and often the limited time in port is devoted to a variety of safety, regulatory and commercial inspections.

The simple piece of colored bunting flown at the stern of the ship displays the flag state, but the choice of registry has implications on a wide range of issues that affect the working lives of seafarers.

NOTES

1. Paris MOU, 2021. *Organisation.* https://www.parismou.org/about-us/organisation. Accessed 2021.
2. ibid.

18

CABOTAGE AND DOMESTIC MARITIME LAW

Working along the Coast

From French *caboter*, 'to sail along the coast', 'cabotage' typically refers to a country's policy restricting transport services along its own coast to protect its own maritime businesses and workers. A 2018 study by Seafarers' Rights International (SRI) found that nearly two-thirds of UN maritime states all over the world in some way favor their own domestic ships in the governance of their respective maritime cabotage trades.[1]

Cabotage in the US

Cabotage legislation is applied differently in each nation to suit its particular circumstances. In the US, the Jones Act stipulates that ships can operate on domestic shipping routes between US ports only if they are owned by US citizens, built-in US shipyards and manned by US citizens or permanent residents.

The Jones Act is section 27 of the Merchant Marine Act of 1920 and was introduced by Senator Wesley Jones of the

State of Washington. The Act was intended to strengthen the American maritime industry and national defense, although the American maritime industry has declined in the 100 years since. The Maritime Administration of the US Department of Transport (MARAD) reported in January 2018 that there are only 100 privately-owned ocean-going self-propelled vessels engaged in domestic trades and only 82 involved in international trade. Notably, they also report that the US-flag share of foreign trade is only 1.54%.

At sea, the Jones Act limits competition and imposes economic constraints on the three critical domestic trade routes between the mainland and Puerto Rico, Alaska and Hawai'i. On the coast proper, the US also has minimal shipping trade compared to other maritime nations. The inland maritime sector, on the other hand, is vibrant, with tug and barge operations on the Mississippi and Ohio rivers and their tributaries and a longstanding Great Lakes fleet feeding iron ore from Minnesota to the Midwest's steel plants.

Many foreign-flag merchant ships still trade along the US coast, but they are prohibited from carrying any cargo between US ports. For example, a car carrier can be fully loaded with 5,000 new Korean cars and then discharge them over a series of US ports and it can also load US export cars at the same ports, but those cars cannot be discharged in other US ports. This restriction results in many ships traveling between US ports in a part-loaded condition when they could be efficiently used to carry cargo as additional freight. The Jones Act blocks any commercial activity in order to utilize this spare capacity for reasons of national protection. Intra-state commerce usually responds by procuring alternative supply chains via road and rail networks, however, transferring the cost burden to the consumer.

Cabotage also affects the cruise industry. Cruise ships based in US ports are typically under a foreign flag and registry, so they are prohibited from carrying passengers directly between US ports. To get around this, cruises make intermediate port calls in other countries: cruises to Alaska stop in Canada, Florida-based cruise ships sail to and from Caribbean ports, and California-based cruise ships sail to and from Mexico.

Cabotage Internationally

Other nations have different forms of cabotage legislation. In Canada, there is no requirement for Canadian ships to be built in Canada, and Canada will issue waivers for foreign-flag ships to be deployed within Canada if there is no Canadian-flag ship available. This approach offers flexibility; only in exceptional cases does the United States issue waivers of the Jones Act.

There is no cabotage regulation within the EU, enabling efficient, low-cost movement of cargo in and around the coasts of Europe. Maritime coastal trade flourishes. The European Commission reports that 75% of the EU's external trade and 37% of its internal trade is by sea. The Commission also gives trucks transporting goods from outside a special waiver that allows them to avoid empty return trips, letting them make a limited number of intra-EU trips. The transport policy of the EU states as follows:

> European Union (EU) transport policy aims to ensure the smooth, efficient, safe, and free movement of people and goods throughout the EU by means of integrated networks using all modes of transport (road, rail, water and air). EU policy also deals with issues as wide-ranging as climate change, passenger rights, clean fuels, and cutting customs-related red tape at ports.[2]

In 2013, China began developing what it calls the 'Belt and Road Initiative' (BRI), a global infrastructure plan that integrates road, rail and maritime transportation into a seamless international network. The target is to complete the network by 2049. China has engaged with 138 countries and is investing in the required infrastructure to develop the supply chains. This is a forward-looking approach to establish a sustainable marketplace supply chain.

The proposed land and maritime corridors of the BRI. https://www.merics.org/en/ merics-analysis/ infographicchina-mapping/ china-mapping/. CC BY-SA 4.0.

The BRI demonstrates how, even when cabotage is local, the supply chain remains global. China views the opportunity to connect the landmass of Asia-Europe-Africa as integral to its long-term economic plan.

Life on Coastal Seas

Work on the coast can be especially intense for seafarers. Port calls can be more frequent, and many coastal ships carry reduced manning, which means increased working hours. Many small ships or coasters working around Europe work a standard 84-hour week, with six hours on and six hours off as the standard watchkeeping system. But the chance to work in a coastal trade also carries some fringe benefits. The route may call at a home port, enabling more frequent visits with family and friends. The coast is less prone to the severe weather experienced on the deep sea and can also have better access to mobile phone reception and the internet.

In the early 1970s I served as the third mate on the *Finnamore Meadow*, one of a large fleet of small ore carriers called the 'BISCO fleet' after the British Iron and Steel Company (BISCO). The ships served multi-year contracts with BISCO and were dispatched to Norway, West Africa and Canada to bring a steady supply of iron ore to the UK. The trade route was ideal for anyone needing a short voyage to make up sea time before their examinations. The ship managers had minimal travel costs for officers joining and leaving at UK ports, and any officer signed on to the ship's articles of agreement could request leave at the next UK port. This was not possible when trading at foreign ports; leave would only be given after a minimum contract period.

Everyone on board the *Finnamore Meadow* liked the tropical weather on the run to West Africa, despite the possibility of stormy weather crossing the Bay of Biscay. Even the run to Norway was pleasant during the endless daylight of the summer season above the Arctic Circle. If the

Finnamore Meadow at South Bank, Middlesborough. Courtesy of LOF News.

Finnamore Meadow received orders to load in Canada, however, there would be a rush of officers giving notice for leave. Nobody wanted to cross the North Atlantic on what everyone considered to be a "rust bucket".

Sadly, the *Meadow*'s reputation was credible. When the ship was in ballast, the ballast water leaked into the cargo holds, and I even observed ballast water leaking through the hull. This meant that the ballast tanks needed to be topped up constantly to keep full. The consensus was that this was fine as long as you were sailing near the coast, because you were within reach of land and rescue.

Cabotage and the *Marine Electric*
The assumption that the coast was safer was also held by

the officers and crew of the US-flag coal carrier SS *Marine Electric* when it was on a regular run transporting coal from Norfolk to Boston. It was a very elderly ship, having begun life 39 years earlier as a T2 tanker in 1944 and later been converted to carry coal. In 1983, the *Marine Electric* sank off the coast of Virginia with only three survivors.

The *Marine Electric*. Public Domain.

It was only at the subsequent marine inquiry that the full extent of the ship's condition was revealed. Unfortunately, the US' policy of favoring American maritime business was partially responsible for old ships like the *Marine Electric* sailing the coast in such poor conditions. The US Coast Guard had contracted out the work of inspection to the shipowner-aligned American Bureau of Shipping, allowing shipowners to squeeze extended years of operation out of aged and deficient ships. Two investigative reporters from the *Philadelphia Inquirer*, Robert Frump and Timothy Dwyer, received the Polk award for reporting on these 'ships of shame' that same year.

In 1984, Capt. Domenic Calicchio was the only experienced merchant mariner serving on the panel of inquiry into the loss of the *Marine Electric*. He campaigned for higher safety standards, including the Coast Guard conducting inspections directly, but came up against resistance from within the Coast Guard hierarchy under Commandant Admiral James Gracey. The significant changes he fought for cost him his career at the time. However, 32 years later the Coast Guard cited him as one of their unsung heroes and named an award after him, describing him as a 'champion of safety'.

Some notable safety improvements resulted from *Marine Electric*. Still, 30 years later, the loss of the *El Faro* between Florida and Puerto Rico revealed that the same circumstances of inadequate inspections had continued to allow substandard ships to trade between American ports. When the Marine Board of Inquiry issued their report into the sinking and loss of the *El Faro* in 2017, Capt. Calicchio would have recognized the recommendations; they were echoes of his own words from 1984.

Sailing along the coast provides an efficient way to move cargo safely at a low cost. Cabotage is a useful but complicated legislative tool: when used creatively, it can protect and promote maritime trade along its nation's coasts, but it cannot come at the expense of safety.

NOTES

1. Seafarers' Rights International, 2018. *Cabotage Laws of the World*. London: Seafarers' Rights International.
2. EUR-Lex. *Summaries of EU Legislation: Transport*. https://eur-lex.europa.eu/summary/chapter/transport.html?root_default=SUM_1_CODED%3D32. Accessed 2021.

19

SEAFARERS' RIGHTS AND THE MARITIME LABOUR CONVENTION 2006

---~~~---

Rules for the 21st Century

Seafarers relaxing in a messroom. David Reid.

Historically, seafarers' terms of employment have been governed and legislated by the flag states of their ships' registries. Maritime nations with long seafaring traditions would issue prescriptive governance outlining how life at sea was to be conducted.

Matters of security and safety on British merchant ships were regulated under the Merchant Shipping Acts, first published in 1834. The legislation included the prescriptive practices to be followed and documentation to keep track of them. Masters were held accountable for following them not just to their shipowners, but to government overseers. Every master went to sea under a certificate of competency issued by the British Government, so for a master to fall foul of the Merchant Shipping Act meant the possible loss of their employability.

Rights of Seamen in respect of Wages.

155. Right to wages, &c. when to begin.
156. Right to recover wages, and salvage not to be forfeited.
157. Wages not to depend on freight.
158. Wages on termination of service by wreck or illness.
159. Wages not to accrue during refusal to work or imprisonment.
160. Forfeiture of wages, &c. of seaman when illness caused by his own default.
161. Costs of procuring punishment may be deducted from wages.
162. Compensation to seamen improperly discharged.
163. Restriction on sale of, and charge upon, wages.

Extract from the 1894 Merchant Shipping Act.

legislation.gov.uk.

Documentation was a very important part of the Acts. According to *More Than a List of Crew*, a research toolkit created by the Maritime History Archive of the Memorial University of Newfoundland, the Merchant Shipping Acts required the master to record the following into the official logbook:

- criminal actions, convictions and imprisonment
- labour offences where prosecution, forfeiture or a fine was intended
- offences punishable under the contract
- a statement on the character of the crew, or a statement declining to report on character
- injury, disease, and their treatment
- all deaths, births and marriages
- all crew who left the ship, other than through death
- the wages due to crewmembers who entered the Royal Navy

- wages and effects of seamen who died during the voyage
- the sale of the effects of deceased seamen and the sum received from it
- collisions with other ships[1]

The official logbook was not the same as the navigation logbook. The official logbook was subject to inspection by the governing authorities, especially the registrar general of shipping and seamen, and masters were questioned about them and required to give explanations. Take this 1911 communication, also provided by *More Than a List of Crew*:

> Dear Sir
> I am sorry having to return my Log + agreement in a mutilated condition but it was caused through Rats getting into the Captain's drawer
> Yours truly
> JH Kewely[2]

Rise of the MLC 2006

Since 1834, the global merchant fleet structure has evolved and flag states have proliferated. Most maritime nations, like Britain, established regulations governing shipping, but the registration of ships in countries with minimal maritime history or governance created an imbalance. In 1948, the International Maritime Organization (IMO) was created as an agency of the United Nations to regulate shipping. The first IMO convention, the International Convention for Safety of Life at Sea (SOLAS) came into force in 1958.

The Maritime Labour Convention 2006, known as the MLC 2006, is the work of the International Labour Organization (ILO), another agency under the United Nations umbrella that deals with workers' rights. Also referred to as the 'seafarer's bill of rights', the MLC 2006 established minimum working and living standards for seafarers working on all ships flying the flag of ratifying countries. This is the explanation provided on the ILO website:

The Convention is comprehensive and sets out, in one place, seafarers' rights to decent working conditions. It covers almost every aspect of their work and life on board including:
   ○ minimum age
   ○ seafarers' employment agreements
   ○ hours of work or rest
   ○ payment of wages
   ○ paid annual leave
   ○ repatriation at the end of contract
   ○ onboard medical care
   ○ the use of licensed private recruitment and placement services
   ○ accommodation, food and catering
   ○ health and safety protection and accident prevention and

○ seafarers' complaint handling

It was designed to be applicable globally, easy to understand, readily updatable and uniformly enforced and will become the "fourth pillar" of the international regulatory regime for quality shipping, complementing the key Conventions of the International Maritime Organization (IMO) dealing with safety and security of ships and protection of the marine environment.[3]

The MLC 2006 first became binding under international law on August 20, 2013. At the time, 30 countries had ratified the legislation. Besides ships flying an MLC 2006-ratifying flag, any ship flying the flag of a non-ratified country is subject to the MLC 2006 when calling at a port in a country where MLC 2006 is ratified and is held to it by port state control checks. According to the ILO, more than 50% of the world's seafarers and 75% of the world's gross tonnage of ships is now covered by MLC 2006.

The MLC 2006 advanced seafarers' rights both as a set of laws and as a political cause in its own right. The Merchant Shipping Acts that had been created by national governments were for regulating the broad spectrum of issues related to the business of ships. Seafarers' rights were there, but only as a section. The MLC 2006 raised seafarers' rights to a global platform and gave visibility to their working and living conditions at sea.

The MLC 2006 is tripartite, meaning that not only

governments and unions but business interests were all driving forces behind it. Quality shipowners wanted some protection against substandard shipowners cutting costs and taking their business. Throughout the ILO website there are constant references to "fair competition" and "a level playing field" for shipowners. Because these quality shipowners already provided decent working conditions, the MLC 2006 benefitted them by holding all other shipowners to the same standards.

Victualling

One important aspect of seafarers' standard of living is the food they are provided. In the 2020 Mission to Seafarers' *Seafarer Happiness Index*, seafarers rated their food at 6.6/10.[4] The Merchant Shipping Acts and MLC 2006 both dedicate specific sections to victualling and provisions. In the 19th- and 20th-century versions of the Merchant Shipping Acts, the quantities and types of provisions were prescribed in detail. The probable reason was that the expense of feeding the crew on a long voyage represented an expense that a shipowner might seek to minimize to the detriment of the seafarer. Provisions had to be part of the law.

On my first ship, the *London Prestige*, I remember reading a poster on the wall with the minimum victualling requirements under the Acts. There was an exhaustive list of food items, each with the quantity required: under 'eggs', it stated that each member of the crew would receive five eggs per week. At two fried eggs for breakfast every day, I could see by my weekly calculations that I was well ahead of the minimum.

In 1967, researchers from the London School of Hygiene and Tropical Medicine conducted a study of nutrition onboard the oil tanker *Esso Newcastle*, which followed the Statutory Scale of Provisions from the 1906 Merchant Shipping Act.[5] The 1906 list was very detailed:

Extract from the 1906 Merchant Shipping Act. legislation.gov.uk.

The team's findings, however, revealed that the Scale of Provisions was out of date and hindered rather than helped the work of the catering department. One of their key concerns was the variability in the quality of provisions sourced from different countries. In particular, they noted that the *Esso Newcastle* had taken supplies of flour at Italian ports. The Italian flour, unlike the British flour the Scale of Provisions had worked with, was unfortified: this meant lower levels of thiamine and niacin, vitamins essential to maintain a proper energy intake. The findings revealed that, despite the prescriptive detail contained in the scale of provisions, there were still more variables to consider.

The MLC 2006 sets forth a less prescriptive approach than the Merchant Shipping Acts. In place of a statutory scale of provisions, it provides a mission statement:

> Regulation 3.2 – Food and catering
>
> Purpose: To ensure that seafarers have access to good quality food and drinking water provided under regulated hygienic conditions
>
> 1. Each Member shall ensure that ships that fly its flag carry on board and serve food and drinking water of appropriate quality, nutritional value and quantity that adequately covers the requirements of the ship and takes into account the differing cultural and religious backgrounds.
> 2. Seafarers on board a ship shall be provided with food free of charge during the period of engagement.
> 3. Seafarers employed as ships' cooks with responsibility for food preparation must be trained and qualified for their position on board ship.[6]

The MLC 2006 covers the entire subject of food and catering in less than 1000 words. In the 1906 Merchant Shipping Act, the narrative and schedule of provisions are twice as long. The authors of MLC 2006, however, recognized that the principle was stronger than the prescription.

The study on the *Esso Newcastle* had revealed the shortcomings of statutory scales of provisions. While the prescription looked good on paper, the provisions could not be issued daily or weekly to each seafarer in practice. Provisions had to be used collectively in the preparation of meals by the ship's cook, so that while five eggs per week per person may have been stipulated, this included eggs used in cooking as well as eggs served for breakfast. MLC 2006 represents a more enlightened and holistic approach to the welfare of seafarers in the 21st century.

NOTES

1. Maritime History Archive, 2011. *More Than a List of Crew Project.* Memorial University of Newfoundland. https://mha.mun.ca/mha/mlc/articles/shipmasters/merchant-shipping-act.php. Accessed 2021.

2. ibid.

3. International Labour Organization. *MLC, 2006: What it is and what it does.* https://www.ilo.org/global/standards/maritime-labour-convention/what-it-does/lang--en/index.htm. Accessed 2021.

4. Happiness at Sea, 2020. 'Q1 2020: A Good Meal More

Important Than Ever'. https://www.happyatsea.org/news/
article/q1-2020-a-good-meal-more-important-than-ever/.
Accessed 2021.

5. T. P. Eddy, Erica Wheeler, and Anne Stock, 1971.
"Nutritional and environmental studies on an ocean-going
oil tanker". *British Journal of Industrial Medicine*, 28 (4), pp.
342-352. https://pubmed.ncbi.nlm.nih.gov/5171426/. Accessed
2021.

6. International Labour Organization, 2006. *Maritime Labour
Convention*.

20

RADIO AND CONNECTING SEAFARERS

Sparks and Marconi Men

British Post Office engineers inspect Marconi's
radio equipment during a demonstration on Flat
Holm Island near the Port of Bristol, England.
British Post Office. CC BY 3.0.

In 1836, the American artist Samuel Morse created the
original Morse code, enabling the transmission of coded
messages over the telegraph system. The telegraph system
became the world's first long-distance communication
system. In 1844, the first telegraph message was sent from
Washington, D.C. to Baltimore, Maryland, and by 1866, a
cable laid on the seabed of the Atlantic Ocean made the first
trans-Atlantic messages possible.

These events occurred after the opening of seafarer
missions on both sides of the Atlantic. George Charles
'Boatswain' Smith had opened a floating chapel for seafarers
on the Thames in 1819, and the Rev. John Ashley had begun
the Bristol Channel Mission in 1839, creating the first model
for ship visiting. In Philadelphia, the Seamen's Church

Institute had opened the doors of its floating chapel to serve the needs of seafarers in 1843.

Today in the 21st century, those of us in maritime ministry are focused on the welfare of seafarers through communication, striving to make a connection with all seafarers that we meet during our ship visits and help them connect with their loved ones at home. Imagine the early days of the seafarer mission, when the only communication system available was the postal service. Airmail would not arrive until the 20th century. Fast ocean liners transported all of the ship's mail along with all international mail. This is the reason for the RMS-prefix; the RMS *Queen Mary* was a 'royal mail ship'. Before the internet, even international phone calls from landlines were costly and were rarely used except in cases of emergency. Posted letters were the main link between seafarers and their families.

Rise of the Radio

For a long period of maritime history, ships left port and remained out of contact until they reached their destination. By the late 19th century Lloyds had established signal stations at Gibraltar, Singapore and any other point of land where ships routinely passed close to shore. As ships passed the Lloyds signal stations, they would communicate by semaphore flags and flashing lamps, and Lloyds could then report the passage of ships to the owners, insurers and charterers. Reports from Lloyds signal stations represented the best that was available in 1880. Radio communication was still over the horizon.

Wireless or radio communication would only arrive in the early 20th century thanks to the pioneering work of Heinrich Hertz, Nicolas Tesla and Guglielmo Marconi, an Italian inventor residing in Great Britain. Hertz began demonstrating the existence of electromagnetic waves in the late 1880s, but was only interested in their theoretical implications. After that, things become more controversial: Tesla invented the Tesla coil, which could transmit electromagnetic waves wirelessly, and presented forward-thinking ideas of wireless communication in 1892 and 1893, but was delayed by a fire that destroyed his laboratory in 1895. Marconi carried forward those concepts and greatly increased the range. Both Tesla and Marconi received patents for radio in 1897, in the US and Britain respectively, and in the years that followed they competed and contested each other's patents bitterly.

Marconi focused his attention on the development of wireless telegraphy for the maritime world, realizing that if he could demonstrate a viable system, there would be no competition. On November 15, 1899, the first onboard wireless telegraphy communication was sent by the American passenger liner *St Paul*. The *St Paul* successfully sent a Morse-code message to an English radio receiver some 66 miles away from the British coastline. The world of maritime communication would change forever. Shipowners rapidly adapted the installation of Marconi's equipment onboard their ships. Marconi would only lease this new equipment, however; the radio officers were known as 'Marconi men' because they were supplied as part of a contract with the Marconi company.

The loss of the RMS *Titanic* on April 15, 1912 proved the value of the Marconi men. The *Titanic* had been fitted with the Marconi radio system, and two young Marconi men, Harold Bride and Jack Philipps, served as the radio officers onboard. They sent out the SOS message by Morse code that enabled the passenger ship *Carpathia* to come to the rescue, saving many lives.

In Morse code, 'S' is represented by three dots and 'O' by three dashes, so the SOS message is '···—···'. Contrary to folk etymology, SOS does not stand for 'save our souls' or anything else; it was chosen because it is straightforward for a novice operator to send on a Morse key. Following the *Titanic* inquiry, legislation was introduced on both sides of the Atlantic to make the provision of wireless telegraphy a mandatory safety provision under the Safety of Life at Sea Convention (SOLAS).

Radio room clocks were different from other ship's clocks. They had two three-minute sections shaded in red, 15-18 minutes and 45-48 minutes into each hour. During these three-minute periods, all radio operators ceased transmitting, switched to the 500kHz distress frequency and listened for any distress calls.

Radio Officers

From the time of the *Titanic* in 1912 until the late 1970s with the launch of global satellites, the role of the ship's radio station remained unchanged. The hardware improved in quality and reliability, but the fundamental system of sending and receiving messages in Morse code remained the same. Radio officers on merchant ships were part of the ship's company and were nicknamed 'sparks' because of the spark-gap transmitters that were initially used to create the signal. Merchant ships only carried a single radio officer, while passenger and military vessels maintained 24-hour coverage with a three-watch system. Sparks had his radio room just behind the wheelhouse, always close to the team navigating the ship.

Radio Office Clock. Courtesy of Roy Gerstner, LOF Radio Officer.

Far from instant communication, the sending and receiving of a message involved a complex series of steps for the sparks:

1. When the shipowner had a message for one of their ships, the message would be sent as a telegram to one of a number of powerful land-based radio stations around the world. For British ships, this was Portishead Radio, callsign GKA.

2. At designated times through the day, the radio station would transmit traffic lists with the unique call signs of any ships for which it had been

telegrammed a message. The ship's radio officer would tune his receiver to the station and listen to hear if his ship was on the traffic list.

3. The next step was to open communication with the station by Morse code. This step was for the radio officer to advise that his ship was ready to receive the message.

4. The station would then initiate the next step by advising the ship's radio officer what number his ship was on the list.

5. The radio officer would then have to wait until his turn to receive the message. Sometimes, this business could take hours, often frustrated by periods when signal strength faded due to atmospheric interference.

6. The actual message would at last come in. Sparks would transcribe the Morse code to words, type up the incoming message and have it handed to the captain.

Once a message had been received, the business of making a reply was the reverse of the steps, requiring sparks to initiate a call back to the station and find a time slot to transmit. In my own seagoing experience, there were times when we were steaming along waiting for orders, perhaps awaiting the name of the discharge port, or instructions about the next voyage. Often, we navigated hundreds of miles in the wrong direction simply because we had not received the message.

The working day for radio officers was different from any other person on board: they typically worked two hours on and two hours off over a 16 hour day. They would adjust their hours to reflect traffic lists and atmospherics. Being a radio officer was a lonely life, spent listening to a constant stream of dots and dashes on headphones. It also required confidentiality: radio officers knew of every communication to and from the ship, so if a message came for a crew member announcing the birth of a child back home, sparks was the first to know. They also knew everything the captain knew.

This confidential relationship between the captain and the radio officer extended to the arrival of the ship's mail. When the agent delivered the large envelope containing everyone's letters from home, the captain would hand the envelope to the radio officer to sort out the official mail from the crew mail. Then the radio officer would act as the ship's postman, bringing the mail to the mess room and calling out the names of those who had received letters. Sparks was the center of all communication.

Routine tasks such as receiving weather forecasts also relied on messages via Morse code. However, these came in a stream of alphanumeric code that the navigating officer would need to decipher and then plot on to the chart. Once plotted, the isobars would be displayed, providing a view of where the low-pressure storms were located. All of these tasks required patience and many man-hours to create.

In 1979, the International Maritime Organization (IMO)

introduced the Global Maritime Distress and Safety System (GMDSS). The new technology brought an end to the need for a radio officer onboard a merchant ship. After 80 years, the wireless telegraphy system pioneered by Marconi using Samuel Morse's code came to an end, and with it the need for sparks. Satellite communications, onboard computers and the creation of INMARSAT to serve the satellite communication needs of shipping led to the loss of an entire department on a merchant ship. Today, the sending and receiving of messages take place instantly, making the world of shipping safer and more productive.

Internet and Conversation

As those in maritime ministry connect with seafarers, they provide the human connection that Cal Newport, the author of *Digital Minimalism*, calls 'conversation-centric communication'.[1] Newport points out that no online experience can compare to the value of actual personal contact experienced sharing a cup of coffee or in a brief one-on-one talk. This is the reason why seafarer chaplaincy remains relevant in the 21st century: the internet has rendered radio obsolete, but it has made personal contact more valuable than ever.

The diminished crew size of today's merchant ship leaves fewer opportunities for social interaction on board. The daily routine becomes one of standing watches, resting and meals. Time in port is kept to a minimum for efficiency and, for the seafarer, it represents increased work: watchkeeping is extended and regulatory inspections such as Port State

Control are conducted, and then there are the routine chores of taking stores onboard. In many cases, the time available to catch a few hours ashore is squeezed to almost zero. This is further exacerbated when port security and transport challenges place tough hurdles between the ship and the rest of the world. Our presence on board to visit and listen to them is reminiscent of the pioneering days of the Bristol Channel Mission in 1839 and just as vital.

When we bring with us a portable WiFi Hotspot, we are bringing the magic of wireless communication that was inspired by the creative imaginations of Tesla and Marconi. Samuel Morse's code has been made redundant by the use of the QWERTY keypad to tap out emails and text messages. The keying of letters to form words, wirelessly transmitted at the speed of light around the world, has placed the tools of communication in the hands of many.

The next time that you find yourself disconnected from the Internet due to an outage or because of a remote location, remember the seafarer who experiences more time disconnected than anyone: the time they have when they are connected is precious.

NOTES

1. Cal Newport, 2019. *Digital Minimalism: Choosing a Focused Life in a Noisy World.* New York: Portfolio.

21

LIGHTHOUSES

Friends of the Seafarer

East Quoddy Head Lighthouse in Campobello
Island, NB, Canada. Courtesy of Nicholas
Nasobkow.

As long as humans have been using ships to travel from

one community to another, those at sea have had to trust in those at shore to show them where they are. The best way to do this before radio was a bright light: presumably the first lighthouses were torches on beaches and bonfires on hills. In recorded history, the most famous tower-like lighthouse structure was the Great Lighthouse or Pharos of Alexandria, from which comes the Spanish word *faro*. The Pharos was built during the reign of Ptolemy II Philadelphus from 280-247 BC, rose more than 100 m and was considered one of the Seven Wonders of the World. Today, the world's coastlines are dotted with more than 21,000 lighthouse structures.[1]

In the early days, the source of the light in a lighthouse was from burning wood or coal. In the 18th century, the Swiss scientist Aimé Argand invented the Argand lamp, which revolutionized the early oil lamps by allowing air to flow around a cylindrical wick, increasing the intensity of the light. The Argand lamp principally used whale oil as the fuel, and this was the standard means of illumination for more than 100 years. By the late 19th century, the first electric lamps were in use, and they were followed by gas lamps. The Swedish Dalén lamp, invented by Gustaf Dalén, was the lamp of choice from the beginning of the 20th century until the 1960s.

Physicists and engineers continued to improve lamps by turning their attention to the development of lenses that could magnify and focus the light. In 1823, the French engineer Augustin-Jean Fresnel created what became known as the 'Fresnel lens'. The first Fresnel lens was installed in the Cordouan Lighthouse at the mouth of the Gironde Estuary, the entry point for the port of Bordeaux on the French Atlantic Coast. The Fresnel lens multiplied the power of the light by four times, so that the light from the Cordouan Lighthouse was visible for more than 20 miles. 200 years later, the Fresnel lens remains in service at many lighthouses.

The ability to focus light enabled the revolving lighthouse beam. This was a critical development, because it allowed each lighthouse to project its own signature. To mariners positioned some distance away from the lighthouse, the light would appear to flash at set intervals, and this discreet code would enable mariners to identify correctly which lighthouse they were observing. As this technology became available, each lighthouse was assigned its unique sequence of flashes, and these were shown on nautical charts. Today, there are 'light list' books that carry the details of every lighthouse, showing their unique light sequences and design. The US Coast Guard has seven volumes of light lists, covering all of the US mainland and territories. The British Admiralty has a complete set of light list volumes covering the whole world.

Lighthouses provide guidance to mariners both by day and night. Many might assume that lighthouses are principally in use for night-time navigation, but by day they are used as place markers to identify a coastline and for navigators to take bearings and establish their position. For this reason, lighthouses are all uniquely designed: they are painted in different colors and patterns. The colors and patterns enable navigators to readily differentiate one lighthouse from another.

Here we need to think back to the era before ships were fitted with satellite positioning systems. When a ship approached the coastline following a long voyage across the open ocean, there was uncertainty concerning the actual location of the ship. Celestial navigation was dependent on being able to take navigational sights with a sextant, but this required clear weather to observe the sun and the stars. On cloudy and overcast days, ships sometimes sailed for several days without the ability to fix their position. The effects of current and weather could place them at variance with what navigators called their 'dead-reckoning' position or DR, their best estimate. Therefore, a navigator approaching the coast during daylight would consult the navigational chart and key landmarks such as lighthouses would be used to confirm the exact position.

Binoculars enabled the markings of a lighthouse to be observed and compared to the light list. On most coastlines, the lighthouses are spaced so that the next one can be seen before the present one disappears from view. This allows the navigator to use them to determine position by taking the compass bearings of both and marking the location of the ship on the chart. At night, the flashes from a lighthouse would identify the unique signature of that light.

For many years, lighthouses were manned by lighthouse keepers, and the construction of lighthouses included living quarters for the lighthouse keeper and his family. The lighthouse keeper kept vigil over the lamp, lens and machinery.

Technology and automation led to the phasing out of almost all keepers. In the US the last manned lighthouse was in Boston in 1998. In the same year, the United Kingdom bade farewell to the last manned lighthouse at the North Foreland in Kent. Canada, however, has retained 51 manned lighthouses for operational reasons in New Brunswick, Newfoundland and British Columbia. Today, many lighthouses are popular tourist attractions and are manned by a new type of lighthouse keepers, usually volunteers, who serve as tour guides and run gift shops and museums.

As a former navigator, I had considered leaving the sea in the 1970s with a possible career as a lighthouse keeper. The task of being the keeper of the light resonated with me because I knew how important it was for the safety of seafarers. Before I could apply, however, automation arrived and the job of a lighthouse keeper vanished from view.

During a business trip to Finland in 2003, our Finnish hosts arranged for us to stay in a lighthouse that had once seen double service as a lighthouse and pilot station. At each level in the high column of the lighthouse, there were bedrooms where pilots had slept while waiting for a ship to pilot. That night, I slept soundly in the Kylmäpihlaja lighthouse dreaming of what might have been had my aspirations of becoming a lighthouse keeper been realized.

Just as lighthouses indicate the way forward for those at sea, lights are often used as symbols of faith and spiritual journeying in scriptures. There is Psalm 119:105, "Your word is a lamp to my feet, and a light to my path"; and John 8:12, "I am the light of the world. Whoever follows me will never walk in darkness but will have the light of life".[2] As chaplains who serve seafarers, the symbolism of the lighthouse and the keeper of the light resonates with our work to deliver a compassionate and caring presence to the seafarers at each of our ports.

NOTES

1. Russ Rowlet. Lighthouse Directory. https://www.ibiblio.org/lighthouse/. Accessed 2021.
2. New Revised Standard Version.

22

VOLUNTEER SOCIETIES AND LEADERSHIP

—∞—

Moral Courage

Sub-Lieut. Ernest Henry Shackleton,
R.N.R, aged 27. CC BY-SA 3.0.

Very few of humankind's noblest achievements, whether in science, politics, art, or welfare, would be possible without volunteers and those who lead them. David Brindle, public services editor for the *Guardian* newspaper, said of volunteering:

> Volunteering has a rich history, traceable in Britain at least back to medieval times when there was a strong association between religion and ministration to the poor and sick. Estimates suggest that more than 500 voluntary hospitals were established in England during the 12th and 13th centuries.[1]

In the same article, Brindle cited a 2001 United Nations general definition of volunteering as work 1) not for financial gain, 2) freely taken up by the worker and 3) for the benefit of someone else. The definition also allowed for flexibility, however, as it is more complex than that: volunteer organizations encourage and thank volunteers in their own ways, and volunteers give of their time and energy for their own reasons. Many full-time chaplains and other non-profit workers have started as volunteers, and many remain volunteers at heart even when it becomes a paid, full-time job. There is also the 'helper's high', a satisfied feeling of having made a difference hopefully well-known to many of us. But all of this goodwill can burn out if it is not nurtured and directed. That is why leadership is so important.

Shackleton: A Leader at Sea

What makes a good leader? Business writer and 'Leadership Guy' Peter Economy said of leadership:

> While a leader's actions may be scrutinized when things are going bad, it is their leadership qualities that shine through the worst of times. It is these same qualities that employees look up to, respect, and work very hard for.[2]

Economy's description of leadership is perfect for the leadership required in the Merchant Navy. The crew looks towards their leadership team on board when the conditions are the worst, and that is what establishes respect for them.

The RRS *Discovery* beside the Victoria and Albert Design Museum in Dundee. David Reid.

British polar explorer and national hero Sir Ernest Shackleton called optimism "true moral courage." After an 11-year career of merchant seafaring, in 1901 Shackleton volunteered to join Capt. Robert Falcon Scott's Antarctic Expedition on the RRS *Discovery*.[3] Despite being turned down at first, Shackleton was accepted to serve as 3rd lieutenant, responsible for stores and stowage of supplies.

When the *Discovery* reached Antarctica, Scott chose Shackleton to join him on the trek to the South Pole. That expedition failed, and Shackleton was sent back part-way through, but the adventure was an awakening for him.

Later, Scott set out without Shackleton on a second expedition with a different crew on the RRS *Terra Nova*. He arrived at the South Pole on January 17, 1912, only to find out that the Norwegian Roald Amundsen had arrived five weeks earlier, and on the challenging trek back to their ship, Scott and his party succumbed to the severe Antarctic conditions and perished.

In 1914, Shackleton led an expedition of his own on the *Endurance*. That expedition failed when the *Endurance* was crushed and sank under the ice pack in the southern winter of 1915. He never achieved his original goals of crossing the whole continent or reaching the South Pole.

Roald Amundsen said about Shackleton, "Courage and willpower can make miracles, I know of no better example than what that man has accomplished." Why did he say that about Shackleton, the apparent failure? Shackleton is revered not because his primary mission succeeded, but because of his leadership when it failed under extreme adversity. Shackleton accepted the sinking of the *Endurance* as a fresh challenge and took on the new mission of getting his crew home safe. To achieve this, he and two of his men took a lifeboat, the *James Caird*, on an incredible 17-day journey to the island of South Georgia. From there Shackleton navigated on foot across the interior of the island to a whaling base and launched a rescue party to save the rest of his crew. To get his men home safe, Shackleton undertook what can fairly be described as one of the most incredible journeys ever, and in that, he succeeded.

In 2001, I read a *New York Times* review of a book written by Margot Morrell and Stephanie Capparell entitled *Shackleton's Way*. I have to admit that in 2001, the name 'Shackleton' was not familiar to me, because the central character associated with the Antarctic had been Scott ever since I learned about his polar expeditions at school.

After reading the review, however, I purchased *Shackleton's Way* and read about Ernest Shackleton. I read about his own experiences as the junior officer on Scott's Antarctic expedition aboard *Discovery* and his epic Antarctic adventure with the *Endurance*. Morrell and Capparell wrote:

> Shackleton made his men want to follow him; he did not force them to do so. In the process, he changed the way his crewmen saw themselves and the world. His work continued to inspire them for as long as they lived and to inspire others around the world long after that. There is no greater tribute to a leader. His tools were humor, generosity, intelligence, strength, and compassion. That's Shackleton's Way.[4]

Shackleton's style of leadership was everything that Robert F. Scott was not. He was indeed a master mariner, but his greatest talent was as a master manager.

In 2006, I was able to complete my personal journey to Antarctica. This enabled me to fulfill two ambitions: to have set foot on all seven continents and to see where Shackleton and his crew were stranded in 1915. Observing Elephant Island brought a vivid reality to everything that I had read about in *Shackleton's Way*.

Moral Leadership

Having taken *Shackleton's Way* to heart in every aspect of my own life over the last 20 years, there are three of his thoughts on leadership that stand out for me as guiding principles:

1. Optimism is true moral courage.
2. Leadership is a fine thing, but it has its penalties. And the greatest penalty is loneliness.
3. I have often marveled at the thin line which separates success from failure.

Serving as a CEO and managing director in my business career, I witnessed all of these principles in action. I know that many times it takes courage to remain optimistic. In more recent years, since I redirected my energy to the pursuit of serving others, I have found that these principles continue to provide valuable guidance as I devote my time to working in the field of chaplaincy.

When I became involved with SCI in Philadelphia and its mission of serving seafarers, I asked myself, "What would Shackleton do?" Shackleton always led by example, never asking anyone to do work he wouldn't do himself. When I helped train volunteer ship visitors, I used these principles to promote the right approach to a ship visit.

Seafarer missions began in Victorian Britain as voluntary societies that used donated money and time to work in narrow spaces. While we have evolved into organized ministries and associations with budgets and staff worldwide, our dependence on people's goodwill has remained the same. Every voluntary society has the constant challenge of keeping a margin capable of supporting its mission, and the key to making it work is effective leadership.

Nonprofits are at risk when their leadership loses focus and strays from the mission. As Shackleton reminds us, there is a fine line between success and failure. Many seafarer missions are challenged to secure funding to maintain services and replenish the team of volunteers. This is where we need Shackleton's 'true moral courage': optimism.

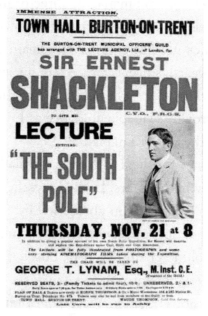

Promotional poster for a lecture tour by Shackleton. Public Domain.

St Christopher's Hospice, founded in 1967 by Dame Cicely Saunders Hospice in Sydenham, Kent, is considered the world's first modern hospice. When I visited the hospice on a trip to London, Joint Chief Executive Shaun O'Leary told us that they needed to raise twenty million dollars each year to maintain their free service. Great Britain has had universal healthcare since 1948, and I was shocked to learn that the National Health Service meets only about 30% of St Christopher's costs. By comparison, in the United States, about 94% of hospice care is borne by Medicare. As I listened to this explanation, I realized that our seafarer missions face the same challenges as St Christopher's, with each year presenting a fresh round of fundraising campaigns to continue the mission.

Listening to Shaun O'Leary, I also recognized how important advocating and providing direction also is. In organizations like hospices and seafarers' ministries, leaders need a unique dedication, because they carry a burden of compassion to those they serve. Just like volunteers, the special people who step forward to be leaders and stewards of voluntary societies require recognition. All of us who are served by their excellent works owe them our thanks.

NOTES

1. David Brindle, 2015. 'A history of the volunteer: how active citizenship became the big society'. *The Guardian.* https://www.theguardian.com/voluntary-sector-network/2015/jun/01/a-history-of-the-volunteer-how-active-

citizenship-became-the-big-society. Accessed 2021.

2. Peter Economy, 2016. 'The 5 Essential Qualities of a Great Leader' *Inc.* https://www.inc.com/peter-economy/ the-5-essential-qualities-of-a-great-leader.html. Accessed 2021.

3. *Discovery* was built in the Scottish Port of Dundee to withstand being crushed by pack ice. The hull had a thickness of 2 ft and was built using multiple layers of different timber species. See the chapter 'Navigation' for more photos. It has been preserved as a museum and can be seen firsthand in Dundee to this day. It sits on the banks of the Tay River, side by side with the stunning new Victoria and Albert Design Museum. I recommend both as monumental works of human thought and craftsmanship.

4. Margot Morrell and Stephanie Capparell, 1998. *Shackleton's Way: Leadership Lessons from the Great Antarctic Explorer.* New York: Penguin.

Conclusion

As I mentioned in the introduction, much of the writing happened before and after I had heart surgery. While I only learned about it two years before the surgery, I had been living with a latent defect in my aortic valve for my entire life. That little defective machine was there opening and closing inside me while I traversed across the oceans and seven continents and through 50 years of maritime history: a total of about 2.7 billion times, by my calculations. I had quite literally trusted it with my life. But it was time for a change yet again.

The oldest maritime vessel recovered is the 'Pesse Canoe', on exhibit in the Drents Museum in the Netherlands. It dates back to c. 8,000 BC. In the 10,000 years since, the art of sailing across oceans has been improved again and again. Celestial navigation was mastered, and reliable clocks were invented to calculate longitude. Ships moved first by their crews' rowing power, then with the winds, then with propellers turned by engines. Even if the chain of command with the master at the top looks similar, the environment it operates in has changed. Crew sizes have shrunk dramatically. Maritime laws have been written and rewritten. Positions like the radio officer have disappeared while the engineers have new technologies to manage. The shipping container has changed cargo handling from manual to machine labor. With satellite-based communication and navigation the flow of information from shore to ship has grown from a trickle to a steady stream.

Seafarers have to embrace change not only onboard but in their global industry. They compare and contrast each port they visit, becoming astute observers of best practice. As a former seafarer, I try to do my part while serving as a chaplain to make their visits to my port a positive experience. Just as seafarers' business is constantly changing, ministries must always be changing along with them. Better that we embrace change.

Indeed, the maritime world is full of people working outside their comfort zones. That was true for me as a cadet boarding my first ship and later as a former chief officer supervising my first port operation. At the end of my commercial career, when I became a volunteer going onboard as a provider of emotional and spiritual support, I was outside my comfort zone again. Indeed, everyone who comes to seafarers' ministry, whether from a maritime background, a religious background, or out of a simple dedication to serving others, is already stepping into new territory.

I hope this book is a help to those who serve seafarers, especially those who are unfamiliar with the many facets of their lifestyle. But I also hope it instills a more general interest in seafarers, their world and their wellbeing. We are all connected to them by the global supply chain, and their work deserves our respect and attention.

APPENDIX: TIMELINE OF DAVID REID'S CAREER

- 1968: Navigating cadet on the *London Prestige*, a bulk carrier carrying scrap steel and grain between the US and across the Pacific.

London Prestige in 1969. Courtesy LOF News.

- 1970: Navigating cadet on the *London Statesman*, a general cargo ship carrying consumer goods, machinery, steel and chemicals between East and Southeast Asia and the US.
- 1971: Third mate on the *Overseas Adventurer*, a tanker carrying oil between Venezuela, Europe and Africa.
- 1971: London & Overseas Freighters' Cadet of the Year.
- 1972: Third mate on the *London Citizen*, a general cargo ship carrying consumer goods, steel and

grain between Canada, the US, Spain and South Africa.

- 1972: Third mate on the *Finnamore Meadow*, an ore carrier carrying iron ore between West Africa, the UK and Norway.

- 1973: Second mate on the *London Statesman* again, this time carrying consumer goods, machinery, raw sugar and grain between Canada, the US, Argentina, West Africa, South Africa, Saudi Arabia and Japan.

- 1974: Joined the Canadian company Upper Lakes Shipping as second mate.

- 1975: Chief mate on the *Ontario Power*, a self-unloader carrying coal, gypsum and iron ore between Canada and the US.

- 1976: Chief mate on the *Phosphore Conveyor*, a self-unloader carrying iron ore and phosphate rock between Venezuela, Canada, the US and Germany.

- 1976: Chief mate on the *St Lawrence Prospector*, carrying grain between Canada and Norway.

- 1976: Chief mate on the *Canadian Transport*, an ore carrier working within Canada.

- 1977: Cargo Superintendent for Troll Carriers, a Canadian/Norwegian joint venture.

- 1978: Operations manager for Leitch Transport, a Canadian deep sea and coastal fleet.

- 1979: Oversaw development of the Navy Island Forest Products Terminal (Forterm) in Saint John,

New
Brunswick.

- 1981: Operations manager for Westport
Navigation, a global operation fleet of chartered
bulk carriers.
- 1984: CEO of Ducal, a stevedoring and ship
chartering company in the Port of Long Beach,
California.
- 1997: CEO and president of Novolog Bucks
County, a new steel terminal in the Port of
Philadelphia,
Pennsylvania.
- 2005: Supply chain director at Teesside Steel
Works in Middlesbrough, North Yorkshire.
- 2016: Chaplain for the Seamen's Church Institute
(SCI) of Philadelphia and South Jersey.
- 2021: Fellow of the Nautical Institute.

ABOUT THE AUTHOR

David Reid served in the British Merchant Navy and the Canadian Merchant Marine for eight years at the rank of Chief Officer. He came ashore to work in the maritime industry of Canada in ship and port operations. After relocating to the United States, he spent forty  years as a business leader in ship chartering, stevedoring, port operations and supply chain management for the steel industry. He is the founder of Shackleton Partners, LLC, a consulting firm serving clients on both sides of the Atlantic for more than 15 years. In later life, David attended seminary, obtaining a master's degree in Interfaith Action. He has served as a volunteer chaplain with the Seamen's Church Institute of Philadelphia & South Jersey.

Also by David Reid

Eight Down: an examination of eight major maritime disasters from the last half-century and the lessons to be learned from them. Available on Amazon.